William Johnston, John Hyslop

Memorial Volume of John Hyslop

The Postman Poet

William Johnston, John Hyslop

Memorial Volume of John Hyslop
The Postman Poet

ISBN/EAN: 9783337777968

Printed in Europe, USA, Canada, Australia, Japan

Cover: Foto ©Thomas Meinert / pixelio.de

More available books at **www.hansebooks.com**

MEMORIAL VOLUME

OF

JOHN HYSLOP,

The Postman Poet.

EDITED BY WILLIAM JOHNSTON.

KILMARNOCK :

J. C. MOTSON, "HERALD" OFFICE, DUKE STREET.

1895.

CONTENTS.

iv.

Preface.

WHEN the postman poet, John Hyslop, was on his death-bed, and realised that the end was drawing near, he requested me to take charge of his literary remains. He had for some time entertained the desire of publishing a second volume of poems, but illness intervened and prevented its fulfilment, so he was specially anxious that, after he was gone, a selection should be made from his fugitive poems—of which there were hundreds, written since the publication of his volume in 1882—and published in volume form. I have endeavoured to carry out the dying wish in the best possible way, and believing that, as he incorporated in his volume several poems written by Mrs Hyslop, it would be only fitting and appropriate that in the memorial volume other poems and stories of hers should appear. From the mass of manuscript, which was written on all sorts and scraps of paper, I have taken what I believed was best calculated to reveal the mind of the author, and most likely to be appreciated by all who knew him either as man or poet. In the work of selection I was willingly aided by Inspector Chalmers, Kilmarnock, himself a writer of pleasing verse. Among the poems in this volume will be found a few that appeared in the volume published in 1882, but with that exception the poems have never hitherto appeared in book form, indeed, some of them till now never were in print. For information as to the life of John and Mrs Hyslop I am indebted to several appreciative articles that appeared in the *Cumnock Express*, *Evening Gazette*, *Modern Scottish Poets*, etc. That John Hyslop was not only a sweet singer, but a prose writer of considerable power, the stories in this volume will prove. While knowing that the work of editing might have been more ably done, I am certain that none could have undertaken it with keener zeal or with a kindlier wish to do lasting honour to the memory of the postman-poet. As there is a widespread desire to raise a fitting monument over the tomb of John Hyslop, I hope that this volume will meet with a ready sale—the proceeds of which will be entirely devoted to that object.

WM. JOHNSTON.

52 JOHN FINNIE STREET,
    KILMARNOCK.

Biographical Sketch of John Hyslop.

The following sketch of the life of John Hyslop is mainly based on autobiographical notes written in 1881, apparently at the request of Mr Murdoch. Our subject was born in a sweetly rural district, in an auld thack biggin', in the little hamlet of Kirkland, in the parish of Glencairn, Dumfries-shire, on the 19th February, 1837. His father then, and for nine years after, was employed by Sir Robert Lawrie of Maxwelton, whose fair ancestress, "Annie Lawrie," will fill a niche for ever in our sweet songs. Hundreds of times in boyhood's merry days John Hyslop gathered bramble berries and poo'd the nuts and slaes, and waded waist-deep amang the brackens and the broom on the bonnie braes of Maxwelton. His father wrought on the home farm and received his own food there, with eight or ten shillings per week as wages. This was not a very magnificent sum with which to keep a house, pay rent, and support a wife and four of a family, of which John was the second. Regarding his mother and the family struggles, John wrote :—"Thank God, she was a true specimen of the sturdy spirit of independence, and when she saw the need buckled tae wi' micht and main to help to keep the family pat a-bilin'." There were no School Boards in those days, and every tot in a man's house had to turn out to work as soon as any sort of job could be found which it was capable of performing. Consequently John Hyslop's education was of the slightest—one year and eight months being all the school education he ever received. At the age of eleven he was put to work in real earnest, and never stopped from that until a few months prior to his death, when he retired on the Post Office pension list. His first employment was that of a walking craw-bogle, herding the birds off the seeds in a nursery during the Spring months—rattling a pair of huge clappers and halooing at them whenever he saw them alight. This sort of work extended from the schreech o' day till the gloamin' fa', yet John Hyslop was happy. Writing of this time he says :—" My spirit was singing its sang wi' the bees and the birds, and dreaming all sorts of impossible dreams of what I would be when I grew to be a man, and went out into the wide, wide world to seek my fortune. These were the times ! Happy the man must be who can keep the boy's heart beating in his bosom to the end of his days. Never did conqueror returning from some well-won victory with a nation's honours showering thick around him march with a prouder heart than did I that sunny Saturday afternoon in Spring when I walked home with the first half-crown I ever earned, and, laying it in my mither's lap, got a kiss frae her and a penny to mysel'." Two years before the time alluded to here, his father had left the employment of Sir Robert Lawrie owing to failing health, and had removed from Kirkland to the village of Thornhill. The family remained there for five years, removing to Kilmarnock at the May term in 1851, and there he ever after resided till his death in 1892. He was a little over fourteen years of age when they arrived in Kilmarnock, and he drifted about at odd jobs—message-boy in a grocer's shop for a year or two, boy with James M'Kie of Burnsiana fame, and " devil " in the printing office there filled up about five years. His parents wished him to learn the engineering trade, and he was therefore duly apprenticed to the firm of Blair & Sons, machine makers and engineers, and there he remained for the space of five years. But not agreeing with the lay and vice, or, perhaps, if the truth must be told, his restless spirit was beating its wings against the four walls of the workshop with an intense yearning to be out once more under the blue canopy of Heaven, away from the noise of the grinding, ceaseless whirling of the wheels, and in hearing once more of the sweet songs o' the laverocks and the linties, so with the far-off billings of their music still echoing in dreams, and the love for rambling among the country lanes he had brought with him into the town, as one of the dearest memories of his boyhood, just as his apprenticeship was finished, hearing of a vacancy in the Post Office, he applied, and was successful, being nominated to the situation of messenger on the 16th March, 1860. This duty he performed for six years, being promoted into the office as stamper at that time. This being a night and day shift alternately, he did not like it, so after working at it for three years, secured a position as letter carrier. He was upwards of thirty years in the employment of the Post Office. Alluding to a dismal time in his family history, John wrote: "My father died in September, 1860, of spotted and putrid fever. A few weeks after his death I was laid down with the same disease, and for many weeks my life was despaired of, but ultimately getting a little better, and just as I was beginning to hirple through the house with a stick, both my mother and my sister were confined to bed with the same trouble. My eldest brother had emigrated in 1854 to Sydney, New South Wales, and my youngest sister having died in 1855, when these two were now laid prostrate with the deadly fever, it comprised our entire household, and there was I, a puir, weak, tottery, rickle o' banes, wandering through the fever-stricken house, and tried as best I could to do the turns of the place, for the neighbours were all afraid to venture in for fear of infection." The circumstances of this severe trial John Hyslop has given in detail in his poem, "The Weary Weird," which he composed in 1870, ten years after the event, and the thoughts which surged through his own brain in the delirium of fever he photographed in "Fever Stricken," which obtained one of the *People's Journal* Christmas competition prizes twenty years after. John was twice married. The first marriage took place in the summer of 1863, when he was in receipt of 11s 6d per week, but odds and ends brought in a shilling or two more. Six children were born to them, three girls and three boys; of whom two girls and one boy died before their mother left his side to join them in the Better Land. After fourteen years of wedded life filled with sunshine and shadow; with smiles and tears; with many struggles and many triumphs, she who had been a loving mother and a good and loyal wife, died in the summer of 1877. Feeling his household getting into disorder, he married again in December of the same year, Sarah Jane Stewart, who had been spoken of to him by his first wife weeks before she died as the one she would like as her successor. Alluding to her, John wrote : "Clever, warm-hearted, and impulsive, widely read, with a magnificent memory, in many things our tastes and feelings are identical, and she, like myself, has been for years a maker of verses, some of which have appeared in various journals. Some of her lines are inscribed along with Surfaceman's, and others in the Poet's Album in Kilmarnock Burns' Monument." John could scarcely tell when he began to write verses, but he was at it for about forty years. Their composition was the solace and comfort of many a leisure hour. Most of his verses were the utterances of his own spirit, as the mood seized him, without straining after effect. Indeed, as he said : "With little care where the winds of heaven might blow the rude, uncultured notes with which

I made a little music to my own soul." He was fond of
dramatic performances from his boyhood, and in his earlier
days ventured on several occasions upon the boards of local
houses, and that with success. All his days he was an
omnivorous reader, and latterly might have been described
as a bookworm. He collected a library, numbering some
700 or 800 volumes of miscellaneous literature, comprising
a few rare old curios. His volume of published poems in
1882 met with considerable success, and gained him the
approbation of competent critics in the Press and in other
literary paths. He had a wide circle of remarkable acquaintances, and knew intimately Alexander Smith, Gerald
Massey, Nicolson, Bob Wanlock, Robert Ford, "The
Surfaceman," who often visited and corresponded with him;
William Shelley of Aberdeen, and many others. At the
celebration of Burns' Centenary of 1859, John Hyslop took
the prize offered by the combined literary associations of
Kilmarnock for the best poem on Burns. On several
occasions he was a prize-taker in the annual Christmas
competitions of the *People's Journal,* and an occasional
contributor for more than twenty years to the local journals
and other periodicals. It was only when physically weak
and feeble that he retired from the postal service; but,
contrary to his own expectations, he lived but a short time
to enjoy his pension, and after a short illness he quietly
passed away on Saturday, 16th April, 1892.

On August 14th, 1891, a few months after retiring from
the Post Office service, the comrades of the postman-poet
in the Kilmarnock Post Office met with him in a social
capacity in the Rainbow Restaurant, and presented him
with a token of their esteem, which consisted of a purse of
money. It will be interesting to many of his friends to
have his speech delivered on that occasion given a perma-

nent place in the Memorial Volume. He said—

There are hours which become epochs in our life's history— hours which all the weal or woe the dim future holds can never erase from the pages of memory's magazine volume. This to me is one of these hours. I can only thank you most heartily for this tangible mark of your esteem. I am positively not aware of anything I have done during my thirty-one years' service among you that rendered me at all deserving of it. Thirty-one years!—that represents a good bit of a man's life-time, and many changes have I seen in the staff since I first entered it. I have served under four postmasters during that time—Mr Rankin, Mr Dickie, Mr Bryson, and our present chief, Mr John Ballantyne. There were only three deliveries by letter-carriers when I began, and now we have five. Post-cards, half-penny stamps, and the parcels post were then things undreamt of. Wages have been nearly doubled during that time. When I began, and for six years after, I was in receipt of the mag- nificent sum of 10s per week without holidays, and I was thirteen years in the Kilmarnock Post Office ere I received £1 a week. Things have altered considerably for the better during that period, as you are aware, and what with the advance in wages and other advantages lately granted you, perhaps the Post Office staff will have reached the end of their grievances before the beginning of the next century. What a crowd of faces I have seen coming and going among the staff during my long service! All the letter- carriers who wrought side by side with me when I first began have gone over to the majority, and in some auld kirkyard or other lie sleeping their last sound sleep. W. Thomson, John Wyllie, John Auld, John Johnston, W. Templeton, A. Hamilton, and many others I could name are all away, and none know who among us may be called on to follow next. I have seen some of the boys who came in amongst us grow up to honourable manhood and settle down in homes of their own, and many more take flight in search of fortune to larger towns or foreign lands. I remember with great pleasure the many happy annual meetings, more especially in the earlier years of my service, when not only the Post Office staff, but the young men employed in the front grocery stores of W. Rankin & Sons, sat down to supper in "Dannie" M'Dougall's, with our post-master, Mr David Rankin, as chairman, while Mr James Blair officiated as croupier. A favourite song of Mr Rankin's was "The Fine Old English Gentleman," while Mr Blair would favour us with a scene from Macklin's "Man of the World." But these reminiscences are running away with me. I rose to thank you for your sensible and most welcome testimonial. I shall never forget that con-siderably more than one-half the years of my life were spent in Kilmarnock Post Office, and that I received many kindnesses from one and all. Though I have now left the service on pension, it does not follow that our friendship for each other should grow less, and I hope to have many happy meetings among you yet. I thank you most heartily for your kindness to me to-night.

His desire of "many happy meetings" was destined to be disappointed, for in eight months he had crossed "the bourne."

We give the following sonnet by Mr John Fullerton, who was a highly-esteemed friend and correspondent of John Hyslop :—

With Spring's first blossom and the song of lark
   The flow'r was shed, and hush'd the song so sweet ;
Lov'd forms and faces seemed so strangely dark ;
   The kindly, tender heart had ceas'd to beat :
   The soul set free to rise on pinions fleet
Above "death's dark vale" and "life's prisoning bars,"
Beyond the sun, beyond the farthest stars,
   Towards the city with the gold-paved street,
   Where, clad in raiment white, the ransom'd meet
"The King upon His Throne." Oh, brother mine,
There thou shalt joy to hear a song of thine
That here had healed, perchance, "some hidden scars,"
   And golden harp in hand for ever raise
   The voice in hallelujahs to Christ's praise.

The Cottage, Pitfour, May, 1892.

I have followed John Hyslop's example as given in his volume of 1882, when he published a few of his wife's poems along with his own. Besides poems, in this volume will be found stories, which serve to show that, even as a novelist, she is possessed of undoubted ability and talent.

Mrs Hyslop was born at Saint Fillans, in Perthshire, beautifully situated at the foot of Loch Earn. Her father, John Stewart, was a soldier in his youth, and served in that capacity for twenty-four years, the greater part of that time being spent abroad. He was in St. Helena during the whole time of Napoleon's captivity. He married before leaving the army, but Sarah Jane was not born until after his discharge, and after he had returned to Loch Earn. She was born about the autumn of 1845. Related to the Stewarts of Advorlick, its then proprietor, unsolicited, procured for her father a police inspectorship at Loch Earn Head, which situation he held until within a few months of his death. With his salary as inspector and a sergeant's pension the father was able to bring up his family of eleven children without the struggle experienced by many parents with large families. Sarah Jane received her early education at Loch Earn Head, and resided there until she had reached the age of twelve years, when she was sent to the Normal School, Glasgow, having early displayed special aptitude for learning. Before she had reached her seventh year she could repeat several old Scotch ballads, and at the age of nine could repeat the Psalms from the 1st on to the 24th without a mistake, and also every line of the 119th. Not long after entering the Normal her mother died, and in a little more than a year afterwards her father was laid in the grave. Writing of this period, she says—"All joy seemed blotted out of my life. I had then to be taken from the Normal School, to which I had been sent after my mother's death, and nothing remained for all of us who were able but to turn out to service. My eldest brother had gone to sea as admiral's clerk, and within a year or two after these sad events, the home we loved so well was for ever closed against the boys and girls who romped and played around its blythesome hearth. After serving in different capacities in several well-to-do families, I was married to John Hyslop in the winter of 1877." As early as her fourteenth year she commenced writing verses, and throughout her life poetry has been the solace and refuge of spare hours. She has said :—"My verses are not like those written by long-headed men, for I just make a dash at them, and scarcely ever give them a second thought or look." Mrs Hyslop sometime after the decease of her husband got a situation with a family in Stirling, and there she is now, feeling comfortable and at home. Like John, Mrs Hyslop was a frequent contributor for years to various journals, and was successful in different competitions. The *People's Friend*, the *People's Journal, Dundee Weekly News*, and the Kilmarnock papers from time to time published poems and stories from her gifted pen.

The Burden of My Song.

HIS harp has but three twangling strings,
   This would-be Poet of our times,
Who will persist in verse to sing,
   And pesters us with endless rhymes.

'Tis true, sir Critic, what you've heard,
   I come to cheer the blind who grope,
Through darken'd ways and sunless days,
   And whisper to them words of Hope.

He sings to us no tales of war,
   He sings of things about our door:
No story tells of lust and greed,
   Done in the gruesome days of yore.

True, I ne'er sung of "glorious war,"
   It's horrors I can only sum;
I hear the groans of murder'd men,
   Above the rolling of the drum.

A

And know there fell some mother's son,
   And that each gurgling shriek and moan
Cries ever through the listening space,
   For justice at the Great White Throne.

I cannot speak high sounding words,
   In praise of fearful crime and sin ;
No braggard words of mine shall stir,
   My brother's blood against his kin.

I see my neighbours staggering on,
   Bow'd down with care, for comfort grope,
And so to cheer them in their grief,
   I sing to them a song of Hope.

When sunrise tints the rosy east,
   I see, beside my wandering way,
The daisies and the buttercups
   Are opening up their lips to pray.

And when the choral anthem swells—
   From wren's chirp to lark's song above,
I know the burden of their song
   Is Love, and so I sing of Love.

And so while life and reason lasts,
   And till my heart to beat shall cease,
The burden of my songs will be
   Of Hope, and Love, and Peace.

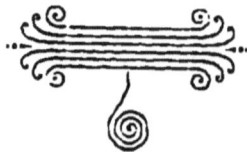

3

The Artist and the Skull.

Time—Evening. A rosy sunset floodeth the Artist's room. Weeks before he had purchased for purposes of his art a dainty female skull. By a strange chain of evidence the knowledge has just dawned on him, it is none other than that of the long-mourned wife of his early manhood. Gazing on it with awe and fear, he thus talks to his own soul :—

"OH, take and hide that thing of fear full fifty
    fathoms deep,
    It's grinning leer is in my dreams and haunts
    me in my sleep ;
Though I have kiss'd a thousand times these lines of
    bleaching bone,
When witching smiles and rosy lips were clothèd thereupon—
But now this ghastly horror comes to taunt and jibe me
    there,
And from beneath the daisy roots creeps to the upper air ;
Yet this white, weird, and mocking thing, this fragmentary
    dole,
Flung from Death's hand to mine, once held a pure and
    spotless soul —
Whose presence in life's darkened ways made sunshine all
    around,
The very spots her footsteps press'd grew consecrated
    ground,
That even yet I strive to trace across time's desert sand—
As pilgrims track the feet of Christ o'er all the Holy Land.

Oh, did'st thou dream for one short hour that I could e'er
    forget thee ?
In mem'ry's hall I built your shrine and there my saint did
    set thee ;

1

Where turning from the strife and dust found on life's
 winding road,
I felt in drawing near to thee that I drew nearer God.
My darling, when you pass'd from me ; for many a weary
 day
My feet were in the thorny paths and on a miry way ;
Our children that we loved so well have long since gone
 from me,
And wander'd down the ways of death till they have come
 to thee.
Now, I have won the wealth and fame for which I toil'd
 so long ;
My name is in the mouths of men familiar as a song ;
But I would gladly give twice-told this pomp of wealth and
 pride
For these old days when we were young, and you were by
 my side.

Poor remnant of the broken cage from which the bird hath
 flown,
That for a few brief months and years I dared to call mine
 own ;
I will not hide thee ; thou shalt watch my goings out
 and in ;
Sweet thoughts of thee will go with me to guide my feet
 from sin ;
And when in hours of quiet calm I bend my knees to pray,
Thy presence here will bear my words to Heaven all the
 way."

So thus for hours the artist rav'd and babbled on the same,
Till at the solemn noon of night God's muffled angel came

And seal'd his lips and whisper'd—"Come, to those you
    love so well;"
Then swiftly as a swooping hawk the shuddering silence
    fell—
And ere the horn of chanticleer proclaim'd a new-born day,
Ice-cold he sat in grand repose, and on his face there lay
The light from that bright land beyond, where she had gone
    before,
And he had the Shekinah seen, and learned the angels'
    lore.

When all the land woke up from sleep, so lusty and so
    strong,
And birds on every quivering bough were bursting into
    song,
Some roist'ring friends, who wish'd still more their revels to
    prolong,
Swept laughing in to know the cause why he had stay'd so
    long.
The light jest died upon their lips; before that awful thing
They stood aghast, and bared their heads as they would to
    a king;
And long and sad in maze of thougnt awe-struck did
    wond'ring stand,
And saw a bleach'd and crumbling skull clutch'd in the
    dead man's hand.

Pity Me!

FATHER, throned among Thy angels,
 Who doth all things hear and see,
Hear my piteous prayer for pardon —
 Pitying Father, pity me!

See, I cling to Thee for succour;
 All things earthly fade and flee:
Let me touch Christ's healing garment —
 Pitying Father, pity me!

Dreams of hope like mists have vanished;
 Gifts of mercy, full and free,
Long by me have been rejected—
 Pitying Father, pity me!

Cankering chains of sin have bound me;
 Make me of Thy freedom free:
Let me drink Thy healing waters —
 Pitying Father, pity me!

Clouds of frowning wrath seem low'ring;
 Clasp me till the shadows flee,
And they melt to floods of sunshine —
 Pitying Father, pity me!

Worn and weary, sad and lonely,
 Let me lose myself in Thee;
Glory, glory, down from Heaven—
 God has stooped to rescue me!

Drifting—Whither?

IN dreams and visions of the night,
    When sleep folds down the weary eyes,
A voice, clear as a trumpet's blast,
    Cried to my list'ning soul—" Arise,
Gird up your loins ; come forth and see
    The sadly dark and tangled maze
That men have wrapt about their deeds
    In these degenerate latter days !"

Then swift methought we twain did stand
    On some cloud-cleaving peak ; and there,
Far as my awe-struck eyes could reach,
    Thick clouds roll'd round us everywhere,
Amid whose folds the thunder growl'd ;
    Like darting snakes the lightning ran :
It seem'd a weird and fearful place—
    Accurs'd of God since time began.

Then slow the curtain of the clouds
    Was parted : silence deep did brood
A little while, then sounds of earth
    Came floating upwards where we stood.
" Pale watcher on this rugged height,
    What see you in the lands below ?"
" I hear and see war's fearsome din,
    And armies marching to and fro.

With shrieks of hate and vengeful yells
    Dense tribes of varied hues and creeds
Rush on till the sad heart of peace
    Doth shrink and shudder at their deeds ;

Grim ghosts of murder'd men sweep past,
  Whose bones rot in the plains below ;
Through roar of guns I hear the neigh
  Of steeds that into battle go.

I see the mangled corpse of one
  Who nobly won the martyr's crown,
Whose deeds, writ in the hearts of men,
  Vie with the knights of old renown ;
There, thick as locusts' treach'rous swarms,
  With glib, smooth speeches learned by rote,
Come fawning with their kiss of peace
  To clutch their neighbours by the throat.

Yon vet'ran, who, through per'lous reefs,
  Would steer the State-ship, Commonweal,
Is marr'd and hinder'd, bit and stung,
  By wasps that buzz about the wheel ;
Loud wrangling statesmen fill the air
  With frothing words and vain debates,
Till, lo ! the cannon of their foes
  Belch out and thunder at their gates.

But, like a rock amidst the storm —
  By tempests gnaw'd, by lightning riven —
Gray Albion rears her dauntless front,
  As deep as hell, as high as heaven.
Yet still more dark the prospect grows ;
  Search east, west, north—look where I may—
There comes no bright'ning streak of light
  To tell the dawning of the day."

*   *   *   *   *

Like feathers in a whirlwind toss'd,
　Awhile my seething senses reel'd,
Then, trembling, woke, and marvel'd much
　The meaning of those scenes reveal'd.
At length, far off from out the depths
　A voice, firm as relentless fate,
While melting into silence, said —
　" God holds the issues—watch and wait !'

The Lone Rider.

Just before the great wave of destruction passed over the town of Johnston, in the terrible floods in America, an unknown horseman galloped through the streets, crying—" Run for your lives !" " Run to the hills !" Some thought a madman had broken loose, but those who heeded his warning were saved. Soon the great wave was upon himself, and he was whirled to his doom with those he had tried in vain to save. No one seemed to know him; he came and vanished with his warning cry—truly "a voice crying in the wilderness." Here was a brave man.

A SHUDDERING wail of horror creeps through all
    our land to-day,
      Our souls have grown so dumb with fear we
    doubt and cannot pray ;
Let others paint these woeful scenes—be mine the task to
    tell
The grand act of a daring man who did a brave deed well.
The wheels of labour buzz'd and droned, the children were
    at play,
And all went well and merrily on in Johnston town that
    day,
When hark ! what awful cry was that ? what rush of
    hurrying feet ?—
An unknown horseman rides in haste down through the
    bustling street.
" Run for your lives !" " Run to the hills !" so ran his
    warning cry,
Then like a whirlwind down the vale swept horse and
    rider by ;
" Run for your lives !" " Run to the hills !" rang all along
    his track,
While close behind the towering wave came thundering at
    his back ;

And awe-struck watchers on the heights soon saw their
tumbling town,
And horse and rider in its path in the great floods swept
down ;
But though his name may ne'er be known to men on earth
below,
God writ it in His Book of Life, and all His angels know.
I have no power with tongue or pen or pencil to portray
That crash of doom, the crumbling town, the thousands
swept away,
I only feebly strive to sketch one brave and Christ-like man,
Who rushing to his open grave rode boldly in the van.
" Run for your lives !" " Run to the hills !" rang out his
warning cry,
And thus to save his neighbours' lives did a brave hero die ;
No deed more daring e'er was done by saint of old renown,
And he has won his laurel wreath, and wears his martyr
crown.
" Run to the hills !" his warning cry rolls on from clime to
clime,
And through the centuries will roll on through all the years
of time ;
Wherever hearts respond like harps when tale of bravery
thrills
Will men repeat his tale who warn'd the people to the hills.

"The Waves are Rising."

A RHYME OF PROGRESS.

"NOW what seek ye here, ye lean curs, with your
snarling ;
Slink back to your kennels, ye vassals and
thralls."
So sneereth "My Lords," yet despite of their
sneering
Our yelpings are heard in St. Stephen's proud
halls.

"My Lords," see ye not that the waves now are rising ?
And those who defiant would stand in their path
The great floods will o'erwhelm, and will suck them below
The whirlpools that seethe from a people's wrath.

Then mount, my good sirs, and ride home to your hunting,
And loll on your Sybarite couches of ease :
But never more strive with the will of a nation,
To tamper or twist with its laws as you please.

The tocsin of doom for your exit has sounded ;
So pack up your baubles and take to the road,
And learn that the strong earnest voice of the people
Is truly and surely the language of God.

See where now " MENE, MENE, TEKEL, UPHARSIN,"
His finger most plainly doth write on the wall ;
Your House that was built upon quicksands of evil
Most surely begins now to totter and fall.

O'er hilltops of wrong sweeps the sunburst of Freedom—
At sight of it's dawning we cannot be dumb,
Then onward, my brothers ! the deeds we are doing
Shall be told by the nations in ages to come.

One Year Ago.

WHEN Spring's crocus month made a gallant show,
I wed my darling one year ago ;
And our psalm of joy took the lark's strong wings—
We knew the beauty of all bright things.

Then the tongue of hope such a brave tale told
Of joys and pleasures so manifold ;
And more deep and strong did our fond loves grow—
In Summer months when the roses blow.

Oft through Autumn woods we would nutting go,
When earth with ripe fruits did overflow ;
And we fear'd no future of grief or pain,
For Eden's days were with us again.

But our months of joy were too bright to last ;
Death's angel came with a biting blast ;
All my hopes were shatter'd and buried low
Where she was laid 'neath the Winter's snow.

And, oh ! now I'm plung'd, since one year ago,
From heights of bliss to the depths of woe ;
But yet all alone I can never be,
Through night's still watches she talks with me.

Now with weary steps through this land I roam,
Till the strong veil'd angel bear me home,
Where, till all my wand'rings on earth are o'er,
She waits for me on the further shore.

Cheer up! Cheer up!

CHEER up! cheer up! ne'er let your heart droop—
  It is folly to despair;
Aye hope for the best, tho' the gathering mist
  Bedims ilka prospect fair;
Tho' dark be the night o' the sorrowful plight,
  And a' seems forsaken and lorn,
The sun will yet rise upon fairer skies,
  And bring a brighter morn.
          Cheer up! cheer up!

Cheer up! cheer up! the earth will not stop
  In its course round the sun,
Nor the sun to shine on the verdure fine
  Ere time was withered and done,
Shedding light—bright light—on the mountain's height,
  Whaur the gloom o' winter lay,
And greenness again on the smiling plain,
  And the bonnie flowers of May.
          Cheer up! cheer up!

Cheer up! cheer up! whispers bright-eyed Hope—
  The real life's fairy queen,
Wha doubles the store at contentment's door
  And aids the Eydent Unseen—
There's aye in the cup a bit and a sup,
  There's wealth for winning, ne'er fear;
There's peace for the mind o' the gentle and kind,
  And health for the hearts o' cheer.
          Cheer up! cheer up!

Cheer up ! cheer up ! brave courage will prop
    The steps o' the weary and lame ;
Like a star in the dark, it guides the lane barque,
    And points to the wanderer's hame.
To the tempest-toss'd there's a stormless coast—
    In the land o' the leal a haven ;
Fause friends may deceive, and fause lovers leave—
    There is truer love in Heaven.
                Cheer up ! cheer up !

Whither?

WE are children by mysteries bounded,
    So little we know,
By strange wonder on wonder surrounded,
    Wherever we go ;
And all things that this great globe inherit,
    From flower unto star,
Hour by hour only tell to our spirit
    How feeble we are.

Though our far-reaching thoughts we keep sending
    On wings of the wind,
Still the darkness before us keeps blending
    With darkness behind ;
But yet sometimes faint glimpses of glory
    Faith cleaves with its sword,
And there gleams from Love's marvellous story
    The face of our Lord.

Till weird lights o'er the darkness keep breaking,
    The mists disappear,
And sin's strongholds are heaving and shaking,
    For dawning is near,
We have built up our strong habitations
    On foam and on sand,
And while vaunting our strength to the nations
    The hour is at hand

When the towers of our boasting will crumble,
    Sure, swift, unawares ;
But God's right hand will lift up the humble
    And winnow the tares.

Soon the loud drums of God will be beating
  The grand *reveille*,
" Wake to judgment " the echoes repeating
  From shore and from sea ;
But, oh, woe should our Judge and All-Father
  Find nothing but leaves,
When He comes in His glory to gather
  And garner His sheaves,

Among the Shadows.

"OII, vanish'd youth! thou green spring-time of life,
    When all our hopes and loves on tip-toe stand,
Girding their armour round them for the strife
    That soon will meet them upon every hand—
When life's pure fountain pours without control
    Its gushing notes, blythe as the bird that sings—
Bright time of roses, when the buoyant soul
    Bathes in the waters of sweet fancyings."

'Twas thus an old man mus'd at close of day,
    While gazing at the slowly setting sun :
The breezes with his thin sere locks did play—
    His day near setting and life's journey run.
" With joy my soul leaps o'er the lapse of years—
    Back to the season when the gay laugh rung
From my glad heart, and busy mem'ry rears
    A mirror of the time when life was young.

From all the dead years sweeps their fun'ral pall —
    Once more I stand within the dear, lov'd spot,
Where from their graves come gathering, one and all,
    Those who once fill'd with glee my parents' cot.
As in the noonday of their life they stood,
    My father and my sainted mother stand ;
Sisters and brothers, in a joyous mood,
    Dance in the dancing sunshine, hand in hand,

My with'ring heart with youthful vigour beats,
    And to the music of their feet keeps time,
Till from my view the vision fair retreats,
    And leaves me basking in life's summer-time.

Now to my side a radiant maiden comes,
  With eyes of hazel; raven locks do curl
Round face and form, where richest beauty blooms,
  And stately as the daughter of an earl.

'Tis the dear partner of my chequer'd life—
  So firm my love had wrapt her round my soul;
Oh, 'twas a blest hour when I called her wife—
  The crowning of my wishes and their goal.
Four pretty children gambol'd round my knee—
  Two brave young boys and two dear comely girls;
The boys possess'd my buoyant spirit free,
  The maids her clear eyes and her raven curls.

But all these now lie in the darksome tomb,
  Where Death, our brother, left them long ago;
And mother Earth hath in her silent womb
  Rock'd them to sleep where I must shortly go.
Each sheltering branch lopt off the parent tree,
  This old trunk's left to brave life's winter storms;
Yet oft in dreams there comes to visit me,
  Out from God's presence, their dear sainted forms.

While I, like miser, hold those moments sweet,
  When fancy's mirror each lov'd form recalls,
Oh, 'tis a time of joy for me to meet
  My grave-strewn friends within fair mem'ry's halls—
For there each spirit of my dead appears;
  I hear them calling from the further shore;
Their voices whisper ever in mine ears,
  'Come, join us here; we have but gone before.' ''

A Plain Man's Creed.

FROM o'er the broad Atlantic's wave,
    From out the fair, wide Western land,
There came sweet words of cheer to-day,
    And clasping of a sister's hand
Which roused me like a trumpet's blast ;
    God keep for aye from care or crime
That sister I may never meet
    On earth, within the bounds of time.

And I can only render praise
    Unto my ever-present God,
Whose spirit gave me words could cheer
    One soul along life's dusty road.
Though strangers both, we fain would know
    If either one be young or old—
The place, and circumstance, of each,
    And if we strive for God or gold.

Among the magnates of the land
    I was not born, but lowlier down ;
I daily earn my daily wage,
    And eat no man's bread but mine own.
I envy no one's rank or state,
    Content I plod my simple way.
A pilgrim in a stranger's land,
    But stepping higher day by day.

I care not for the loud debates,
    Nor windy strife of creeds or school ;
I do not mutter prayers by rote,
    Nor beck, nor bend my knees by rule.

I hold my soul up like a cup,
 High heavenwards, for full well I know
That God will shower His blessings down,
 And that my cup will overflow.

The yearnings of the earnest soul,
 The up-turn'd eye, the waiting hand,
Are language which " Our Father " God
 Doth clear and fully understand.
Through all life's strange and varied scenes
 Where circumstance doth make or mar,
They who hold firm the hand of Christ,
 From God can never wander far.

I do not mean that we should sit
 In silence or with idle hand,
When there is earnest work to do
 On sea or shore, in ev'ry land.
And if we see our neighbour walk
 In paths where sin lures to betray,
Be ours the task to win them back,
 And point them to the Better Way.

Let bigots shriek " Believe *my* creed,
 Or ye had better ne'er been born "—
Those planted on the Living Rock
 Can laugh such bitter words to scorn.
'Tis but their zeal speaks ;—well I know
 We're crowding to the self-same goal
God never yet barr'd Heaven's gate
 On any earnest trusting sou

When some full-freighted barque of hope
    In shatter'd wreck and ruin lies,
We cannot see the Guiding Hand
    While muffled in such fierce disguise ;
But when my stubborn reason fails
    Some hidden mystery to perceive,
My spirit, bending like a child,
    Can only whisper, "I believe."

Because I do not understand,
    I dare not say—"This is not so ;"
In fullness of God's fuller time,
    His wider knowledge yet will grow.
I cannot read the flowers or stars,
    Nor what the bird sings on the tree,
Yet these are revelations strong
    As any prophet's voice to me.

I know that through the gates of death
    Our Elder Brother went before,
And past the gloom of crowding mists
    Will lead us on through Heaven's door
And if we keep our garments clean
    And spotless, o'er life's miry road,
We yet may meet, dear sister, there,
    Within the City of our God.

My Winsome Nell.

'TWAS when swallows on the wing
 Jouk'd an' danced their jingo-ring,
 As ae bonnie nicht in Spring,
                I gaed roaming
 Doon beside the Pear Tree Well—
 There I met my winsome Nell,
 Singing saftly to hersel'
                In the gloaming.

An' when Simmer cam' wi' floo'rs
 An' her honeysuckle bow'rs,
 Aft through sunset's rosy hours
                We gaed weaving
 The bricht wab o' luve sae sweet,
 A' sae firm an' sae complete,
 That twa souls in ane did meet,
                Firm believing.

Sune doon through the rustling lanes
 Will come wealth o' fruits an' grains,
 An' the merry harvest swains
                Lauching cheerie ;
 But the Autumn months will bring
 Juist ae ither fairy thing,
 A sweet denty wadding ring
                For my dearie.

Then when life's dour Winter cauld
 Snaws oor pows or pooks them bauld,
 Sweet wee gran' bairns young and yauld
                May be speiling

On our knees to coo an' kiss ;
But it's lang to that frae this,
Yet sic dreams through present bliss
        Will keep stealing.

But while sun an' mune endures,
Through a' times fleet-fitted hours,
Hearts as firm an' fond as oors
        Will gang roaming
Through the bonnie wuds an' dells,
An' led by luve's witching spells
Walk as ance we did oorsel's
        In the gloaming.

Through Storm to Calm.

MID storm and tempest, through the night,
　　I once a weary way did go,
　Chill'd to the bone with soaking sleet,
　　Fierce, pelting hail and swirling snow ;
　And, blind and dazed, I stumbled on—
　　No star peep'd through night's ebon cloud —
　I felt the fingers of the storm
　　Were swiftly weaving me a shroud.

　But, staggering near the caves of death,
　　Some cherub sweet did surely say—
" Look up, sad heart—night's darkest hour
　　Is just before the break of day."
All through that fearful time my soul
　　In vain had groped for outward sign,
But now these cheering words of hope
　　Swept tingling through my veins like wine.

And, lo ! across the far hill-tops,
　　Night's curtains slowly were withdrawn ;
Like skulking thieves the shadows fled
　　Before the glories of the dawn ;
The snows were melting from the hills ;
　　The tempest and the night were done ;
My psalm on wings of prayer sped up
　　With soaring larks to greet the sun.

Oh, friends, who, compassed round with grief,
　　Keep groping in the darken'd ways,
Who see no pitying stars above,
　　Nor comfort in your weary days —

Look up ! once o'er this woeful road
  Our Elder Brother went before,
Beneath the shadow of whose Cross
  We bend to worship and adore.

E'en now, o'er all the list'ning land
  The herald angels' anthem swells —
"To us this day a Child is born"
  Is pealing from the Christmas bells.
Lean out the trusting car of faith
  And you will surely hear them say—
"Sad heart look up—night's darkest hour
  Is just before the break of day."

And past these days of mist and rain,
  The birds again their songs will sing ;
The flowers lie sleeping in the earth,
  Will blossom in the bowers of Spring ;
So, while the better times draw near,
  For all sad hearts in truth we pray —
"May larger hope and stronger faith
  Come with the coming New-Year's Day."

Hearing the Thunder.

OH ! that words like swords could flash from my pen,
  Where the weak war with the stronger !
Oh ! sisters, brothers, be women and men,
  And snakes and wolves no longer.
Though you vaunt and boast of your noble birth,
  Poor pride-pamper'd Sir or Madam,
Yet your parents and mine once till'd the earth,
  And their names were Eve and Adam.

Ere the trembling sword of stern Justice smites,
  'Twere well we should pause and ponder ;
How woefully mean seem our spleens and spites
  To the angels watching Yonder.
If but seeds of sin and hypocrite prayers
  We give to the whirlwind's keeping,
Oh ! what else can be found save weeds and tares,
  In the day of God's fearful reaping ?

Though the birds now sing and the fountains leap,
  And the lambs skip through the meadows,
Yet the fierce tornadoes now growl in their sleep
  From their cave of gruesome shadows.
Soon from mazes of lust, where ye loll and rove,
  Ye will hear with fear and wonder
The dread Cyclops forging the bolts of Jove,
  And the rolling drums of thunder.

Vain tinsel and gauds from the proud heads all
  God's keen sword of wrath will shiver ;
And smiters of men will stagger and fall,
  To where none will say " Deliver !"

While the low and meek, from their ransom'd place,
    With tempests of song keep telling
Of the marv'llous power of redeeming grace,
    Safe within their Father's dwelling.

Though Wisdom now beckons, and talks through tears
    With a thousand witching voices,
Her words fall unheeded where no one hears
    For din of self's jangling noises.
Still within, without, and all round about,
    We Eternity's seed keep sowing,
Whose fruit shall be known when the years die out
    And the trump of doom is blowing.

Oh, Tempora! Oh, Mores!

(Dedicated to EDMUND YATES, *the " Looker-on in London.")*

THE pæons wild and songs of praise,
    The loud huzzas for victory won
I dare not raise—my heart is sad,
    Oh, brothers, for this deed ye've done.
I cannot hear the victory shouts —
    I only hear the shrieks that rise
From murder'd men ; the air is fill'd
    With widows' wails and orphans' cries.

Oh, man of plots, who rode red-shod
    O'er mangled neighbours to a throne,
The wolves are crouching in your path :
    The day of reckoning draweth on !
Home, poor pride-dandled puppet-prince,
    Play marbles and leap-frog with boys ;
Hence with your " baptism of fire,"
    And blasphemy of frothy noise.

And Bismarck—wily, shuffling Count,
    Who makes in part this blood to flow—
Think you from this red rain of death
    That any lasting good can grow ?
The German fights for Fatherland,
    He says ; he's but the Prussians' tool,
And might fare better—hardly worse—
    Though bending to the Frenchman's rule.

But ye are fools and madmen all—
   Blind wrestlers in the dark that grope
With all the God trod under foot,
   And all the devil at the top.
Oh, bare Thine arm, Almighty Power,
   And bid these woeful wranglings cease !
Oh, haste the end - our souls flow out
   With moanings for a dawn of peace !

A Waiting Soul.

ALONE soul, waiting at life's furthest edge,
   Where deep and far death's realm of terror lay,
Through grief's hushed sobbings heard the voice of
      God
      Call from the darkness, " Daughter, come away."
Then, while night's demons, huddling mute with fear,
   The awful voice of the Creator knew,
A hand of glory smote the clouds in twain,
   And marvellous wonders of weird beauty grew.

The voice spoke on : " Here through your night of pain
   The low, sad burden of your moanings rise,
But see where, upward through a flowery land,
   The pleasant pathway to My kingdom lies.
' Be of good cheer '—lift those far-dreaming eyes—
   Ye grope no longer in the dark alone :
My waiting angels compass thee about,
   And they will guard and safely guide you on."

" Lord, Thou hast called me and I come," she said,
   Then like a lily bowed her weary head
Safe on the bosom of the pitying Christ,
   And friends and neighbours whispered " She is dead."
But from that chrysalis state of seeming death
   The soul that waited had found winnowing wings,
And her poor garments had grown grander far
   Than e'er were wrapped about the loins of kings.
And as they pass'd the burnish'd gates of beryl,
   In richer tones heaven's harpers, clear and strong,
With notes of joy for one more soul redeem'd,
   Broke forth in gushing ecstasies of song.

They put the saint's sweet psalm within her mouth :
Now, free from earthly pain or blight of tears,
Her swelling anthem near " the great white throne "
Flows on for ever through the endless years.

*　*　*　*　*　*

Faint and far off, like music heard in dreams,
From the bleak land she left a chorus swells—
" Glory to God, to us a Child is born,"
Was peal'd and shaken from the Christmas bells.

Sunset.

'TWAS when the sun crept downward to the rim
Of the round world, and from their hiding-place
Came the long troops of shadows, weird and grim,
With busy fingers to hide up the face
Of the dead day—I, in that mystic hour,
Went wand'ring through the balmy fields of June,
Where the gray owlet, from her ivied bower,
Hooted a welcome to the white-faced moon ;

While, flowing through the black and ebony bars,
Wave upon wave, came the long lines of light
Flung from the marv'lous wonder of the stars,
Garlands of worlds twined round the brow of night.
Across the mystery of life's warps and woof
My thoughts surged onward in a dream sublime ;
"What star," my soul said, "in that golden roof
Shall be thy Eden in God's fuller time ?"

Only a Beggar.

A POOR man, raggèd and lonely,
　　Dropt down in the street one day ;
" Oh, 'tis nought but a poor beggar only,
　　A lady in silks did say ;
" And they're thievish and loathsome knaves,
　　Who pester us night and day—
We could spare them an acre for graves,
　　If they'd crawl to them out of our way."

Harsh words these—they cut like a knife—
　　And cruel, my lady, indeed ;
For this poor man was crippled for life
　　When he once stopped your runaway steed.
But for him whom you now grudge a crust,
　　Proud dame, in your trappings so rare,
The rank mould of the graveyard dust
　　Would be dimming the gold of your hair.

Some scraps that you saved from your hounds
　　You sent to his hovel next day ;
And some wine, too, you left on your rounds,
　　In a Dorcas Society way.
But Time's snows are abroad on his brow ;
　　He is palsied in every limb ;
And the fingers of destiny now
　　Have number'd the hours for him.

From the filth of the miry ways,
    Oh, lift him and give from your store ;
He is nearing the end of his days,
    And his pilgrimage soon will be o'er.
So the Master of All you may please,
    And your own end the sweeter will be—
" Forasmuch as ye did it to one of these,
    Ye have done it unto Me."

In Dreams and Visions.

A STRANGE voice hail'd my spirit one day,
In a tone that commanded to stay,
From the mists that had grown,
Where I wander'd alone,
And these were the words it did say—

"Oh, listen ! Oh, hearken and hear !
Where the footsteps of Doom draweth near ;
Men are sharpening the sword and the spear,
And the trampling of armies I hear ;
Oh ! the vultures will fatten, I fear,
'Ere the end of this terrible year."

Then a hand rolled the thick mists away,
And in dark Armaggedon that day
Lo ! an army more numerous lay
Than the motes in the sunbeams that play,
And the clarions and trumpets did bray,
And the drums beat the signal to slay.

Then did cannon to cannon reply,
Till in heaps the dead warriors did lie ;
And the thick air grew heavy with groans,
And the burning and breaking of thrones,
And all things into ruin seemed hurl'd,
As if here lay the end of the world.

For the lion had leapt from his lair,
And in death grips now hugg'd with the bear ;
And the cobras from India were there,
So deadly, so treacherous, and fair ;
Shrieks from German's and Frank's filled the air,
And no man did pity or spare.

And the heaven's above me seem'd brass,
While my spirit cried—" Lord, let it pass,
Bid this terrible carnage to cease,
Oh, send Thy Millenium of peace ;
My brain throbs with fear—I grow blind,
With tears for the crimes of my kind.

Then as swiftly it faded from sight,
As a vision or dream of the night.
From each tree top gush'd anthems of song,
Streams tinkled and babbled along ;
In the still glen the young lambs were grazing
By the loch side the dun deer stood gazing ;
And Beauty was walking abroad,
Fair and fresh from the fingers of God,
But it seem'd, through the shuddering air,
Crept a strange voice that whisper'd—" Prepare."

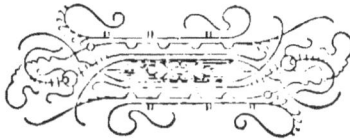

The Golden Calf.

SEE! Fitz Noodle draws near, Lord of hill and glen,
    With his stutter and leering laugh;
Though he never could fill any place among men,
    They must bend to this Golden Calf.
Bow low to the Golden Calf—and pray,
    And flatter, and cringe, and crawl,
Till their backs are bent and their hair grows grey,
    And in pauper graves they fall.

For his ancestors came to our shame and grief,
    Eight hundred years ago;
And through our land, with the Norman thief
    Did like swarming locusts go;
For they harried and slew, and graveyards grew
    Wherever they pass'd along;
And the weak fell like straw, as they ever do,
    Beneath the flails of the strong.

They boast their descent from this Norman line,
    These Lords to whom we pray
For leave to dig in their field or mine,
    For a crust by night and day.
And their harsh deeds search us like grief or flames;
    We are born thralls—fetter'd and bound—
Who must sweat and slave for their lusts and shames,
    And fare worse than their horse or hound.

Though the summer fields may be filled with flowers,
    And the hedges with roses sweet,
We must burrow like moles through the sunny hours
    Underneath our master's feet.

Oh ! God, must Thy stewards before Thy sight
   Do for ever a cursèd thing ?
Will the wrong seem right by the force of might,
   Till Eternity's bells shall ring ?

Oh, no, for that ominous earthquake sound,
   May well make them shiver with fear ;
For the storm and the vultures are gath'ring round,
   And the thunderbolts are near.
And we who faint and fall down by the way,
   'Neath the grinding wheels of wrong ;
Can only stretch hands unto Thee and pray—
   " How long, oh Lord ? how long ?"

Going Back.

AN ALPHABETICAL ACROSTIC.

ALL day I had been wand'ring far,
　By flinty roads, o'er hill and lea ;
Cares gnaw'd my heart, and many a scar
　Dealt by the unkindly fates to me.
Each hedgerow, bent with bursting flowers,
　From ev'ry twig the birds did sing ;
Great joy fill'd all—the laughing hours
　Had brought once more the gladsome Spring.

In pensive mood while I did stray,
　Just as I near'd my native town,
Keen winds did swirl the dusty way,
　Loud patt'ring rain came pelting down.
Months, years, had pass'd, and I had seen
　No friend I'd loved, nor kith nor kin ;
On many a stranger's shore I'd been,
　Pride wall'd me round, without, within.

" Queen of my heart where bide ye now,
　Rose leaf I tost upon the stream,
Shall we e'er meet, and when, or how ?"
　Thus on I walk'd as in a dream.
" Ungodly thoughts long since have died,
　Vain are the joys from fame doth grow ;
Wife, friends, and children by our side,
　'Xcells all else on earth below.
Ye gods ! bring back to me young manhood's prime
Zeal for my kind shall guide life's ev'ning time."

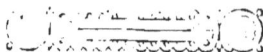

Brave Flora.

WHEN the gloaming fell on Drummossie Muir
    Owre a scene o' dread an' o' fear,
Like chaff on the win' a handfu' o' men
    Had gane fleeing baith far an' near;
But whaur awa' noo was the Bonnie Prince
    They had spilt their best lives to save?
Gangs he hale an' weel, or has he been clutch'd
    In the maw o' the greedy grave?

Oh, he's skulking oot on the bleak hill-sides
    Wi' a lassie to guide him noo,
An' prove ance mair for the ane that they love,
    What a woman will daur an' do.
" Owre my loyal clans," Bonnie Charlie sabb'd,
    " The red hooves o' the spoilers go;
Oh! that wi' them I were streekit the nicht,
    Whaur noo they are lying sae low."

While slowly they crept amang wuds an' caves,
    She wi' comforting words wad say—
" Lean yer weary heid on my lap, my Prince,
    An' sleep safe till the break o' day;
For afore the hunters cud strike ye doon,
    Or that you should yer life bluid tine,
They first shall drain the last draps frae my heart,
    An' maun lapper their hauns in mine."

An' for mony a weary day an' nicht,
    While his foemen sair press'd him roun',
He row'd himsel' up in his tartan plaid,
    An' on rough heather bed slept soun'.

Sae for weeks an' months amid danger's dire
  Bonnie Flora ne'er left his side
Till the ship wi' him gaed booing frae sicht
  Owre the rim o' the frothing tide.

Thus vanish'd the last o' the Stewart race
  Frae auld Scotland for evermair ;
But mony a day frae the harried glens
  Cam' a wailing an' moaning sair ;
For as few o' the brave braw lads gaed back,
  As cam' frae the rout o' Flodden,
For maist ane an' a' bow'd their heids in death
  On the red field at Culloden.

But when leal true hearts in the years to come
  Seek brave deeds on our scroll o' Fame,
In the foremost front o' oor bravest brave,
  They'll find Flora M'Donald's name.

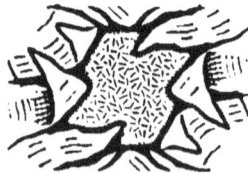

"I Cannot Make My Mind Sit Down."

Suggested on hearing Lord Rosebery in his speech at the unveiling
of the Reformers' Monument, Kilmarnock, relate an anecdote
of a little girl of his who told her nurse " She could not sleep,
she dreamed so much at night." Her nurse said—" You must
not think so much." On telling this to her father, the little one
said—" But I cannot help thinking, papa; I cannot make my
mind sit down." To that young lady I dedicate these lines.

DREAM on, wee meditating Miss—
　　Your words are wiser than you know:
From active, restless minds like yours
　　The deeds that move the world do grow.
They who through battles fierce have won
　　The victor's wreath, the martyr's crown,
Were dreamers who wrought out their dreams,
　　And could not make their minds sit down.

Your father bears his torch of truth
　　Where moral victories may be won:
God grant him length of healthful days
　　To end what he has well begun.
The germs of thought he holds ere long
　　Will blossom into fruitful deeds—
He holds the power to bend men's minds
　　As strong winds bend the swaying reeds.

Though wealth and plenty crown your board
　　And life moves in a pleasant place,
God meant not you should fold your hands;
　　The drones are but the land's disgrace.
Ere long in fashion's giddy ranks
　　A foremost place you well may claim
Think then some hopeless sister-souls
　　For want are drifting into shame.

Where famine rends the poor like wolves,
  And starving children cry for food,
Oh! let them say "She holds her wealth
  But as the means for doing good.
To save from sin my lady deems
  Her robe of glory and her crown;
She lives a pure and noble life,
  And cannot make her mind sit down."

Some time, perchance, before you go
  To mingle with life's busy throng,
Our dainty maid may pause to sift
  The words of wisdom from my song.
I know on all this teeming earth
  There lives not one so great or small
But holds Love's cord that binds us firm
  To God, who is above us all.

The Lanely Auld Wife.

HERE I sit, and my wee wheel keeps turning,
    An' striving to spin an' to pray,
But it's lang frae the first skreigh o' morning
    To the end o' the gloaming sae gray ;
An' though little I get for my spinning—
    Let them cock up their noddles wha daur—
What I leeve on is a' my ain winning,
    And they're thieves that dae onything waur.

Yet I'm blythe and contented as onie,
    I've a penny to hain an' to spen'
An' to dae't at my age there's no' monie,
    For I'm noo past my three score an' ten.
Aye the bite an' the brat's been provided
    By the bountiful Giver for me ;
By His haun' I've been guarded and guided,
    An' will be till the day that I dee.

Sae I croon to mysel' while I'm spinning
    Some lilt o' the days ha'e gane bye,
When, a bare-fitted lass, I was rinning,
    An' herding the sheep and the kye ;
Till I hear the lark pouring and shaking
    Its sang frae the heart o' the cluds,
While the birds a' aroon' me are making
    An anthem o' praise in the wuds.

An' like clear siller bells they seem chiming,
    Thae birds' sangs I never can tyne ;
On my sweet harp o' mem'ry their rhyming
    Comes doon frae the days o' lang syne ;

But further than larks sang an' higher
   Soars upward my fragment o' praise,
Till I speil to my height o' desire
   At the end o' my desolate days.

Whiles the skreighin' win' doon the lang loanin'
   Comes groanin' like some ane in pain,
Till my croon tak's the soon' o' its moanin',
   An' I feel, oh, sae eerie my lane.
Then I stop my wee wheel, an' I ponder;
   An' lost voices hear, for I ken
That my freens' wait an' watch for me yonder,
   When this pilgrimage comes to an en'.

A' the fowk that I ance lo'ed sae dearly
   Ha'e been lifted an' ta'en frae my side
An' I feel my ain limpin' feet nearly
   Noo touchin' the edge o' the tide,
That will bear me awa' like a blossom
   Afloat on the briest o' a stream,
Owre the waters o' Death to the bosom
   O' God, in the land o' my dream.

An' nearer, aye near, an' mair steady,
   The lichts o' His city I see;
Let Him come when He likes, for I'm ready,
   An' few will cry "dool" when I dee.
Sune like south win's that scarce stir the barley
   His messenger saftly will steal,
An' steek my auld een without parley,
   While croonin' my sang at my wheel.

Our Lady Bountiful!

Lines to the Honourable Dowager Lady Howard de Walden on her princely gift to the Kilmarnock Infirmary, for the benefit of the little ones.

" FORBID them not," the loving Master said,
      When little children clamber'd round His knees ;
  " They who would see my Father's face or Mine
      In glory, must become like one of these."

And the same love that fill'd this heart of love
    Set in your thoughts some helpless little one ;
We loved you, lady, from your coming first—
    We love you doubly for the deed you've done.

And on, and on, through all the coming years
    The little ones—the weak, the maim'd, the lame—
Will bless you for the sunshine you have made,
    And praise and honour the De Walden's name.

With gratitude we take your princely gift,
    And tender you our meed of thanks and praise ;
God grant you, lady, in your sunset years,
    Sweet health and pleasure through life's flow'ry ways.

John Stuart Blackie.

SINCE "rusty, crusty Christopher"
   Smote shams with weight of words and pen,
No truer Scot has trod our land—
   A *man* among ten thousand men;
Wherever Scot had wrongs to right
   Your sword of wrath swept flashing there,
Till shams of creed or cruel deed
   Became a hissing everywhere.

And we have heard your words to-night—
   "Words of a dreamer," some may say—
So spake men of the seers of old
   And prophets of the earlier day.
Press onward with your torch of truth,
   Pass up and onward in the van;
All earnest words of honest truth
   Bring near the brotherhood of man.

Manipur.

STRIKE now, my muse, a martial strain with roll of
    muffled drums,
      See where the sad, grief-laden dame, dower'd round
        with honour, comes
To sit within her darkened home, and mourn her early
    dead ;
Oh ! pitying Father, shower Thy balms of healing on her
    head
Who, late within the gap of death, stood staunch, and
    firm, and true,
And proved once more in hour of need what one brave
    heart can do.

Vain now to whisper "Shame," or blame those men of
    proven steel,
Who rushed through treachery to their fates, mayhap
    through over-zeal ;
God holds the record in His hand who first struck
    treach'rous blow,
And weighs within His balance true the deeds of friend or
    foe.

Sore-tested soul, 'twixt fears for " Frank " and love for all
    your kind,
Who nursed the sick, and planned the deed that grew
    within your mind ;
Who, when men quail'd, and hope seemed dead, led forth
    your faithful band
Safe over danger's fearful path and through an enemy's
    land,

D

Now on and on through all the years, while this old earth
    spins round,
Till quick and dead alike shall hear the last trump's awful
    sound,
We'll keep from time's corroding rust, graved on the scroll
    of fame,
In our front rank of bravest brave, sweet Mrs. Grimwood's
    name.

What the Savage Saw.

THE Great Prince Salambo came here one day,
  From his kingdom of Chickeraboo ;
And he thought the whole world turn'd upside down,
  Such rare wonders did meet his view.

For our civilization in vain he sought,
  Both through city and country town ;
As marvelling much, on a fruitless quest,
  He went wandering up and down.

For he saw the toilers who earn'd the gold,
  Like starv'd rats in the gutters die ;
While those who never had wrought for a crust,
  In the robes of their pride sweep by.

And tinsel and tatters drifting apart,
  To the end of opposite poles :
For the rich cared more for their yelping curs,
  Than they did for their neighbours' souls.

For the far-off heathen, he saw them give
  Gifts of gold from their hoarded stores ;
But they hounded dogs at the beggar brats,
  And the heathen about their doors.

And he heard full many in streets and lanes,
  Who did " Holiness " shriek and cry ;
But whose souls were festering sloughs of sin,
  And their lives were a living lie :

For turn right or left, he with wonder saw
   Such lewd women and wolfish men;
The spot should have been a garden of God's,
   They had turn'd to a Devil's den.

Then Salambo, the savage, said—"Alas!
   That I ever such sights should see;
I am sick of this game of knaves and fools,
   And this land is no place for me.

I had rather dwell on the loneliest peak,
   Or in woods with the wolves and bears;
Than crawl into Heaven, through filth and slime,
   O'er the hypocrite's bridge of prayers."

Then shaking, with scorn, the dust from his feet,
   He pass'd onward his lonely way:
But the ceaseless racket roars round us still,
   And will do till the Judgment day.

The Nodding Lillies.

OH, but boyhood scenes are fair, an' just braw beyond compare,
  An' oft memory lifts me back as in a dream
To the woods o' nuts an' slaes, an' ower fern an' heather braes
  To where lillies nodded at me frae the stream.
Though it's forty years an' mair since my feet hae wandered there,
  An' though I ne'er hae seen ae glint o' them sin syne,
Yet sae lang's I've breath to draw, they can never fade awa',
  Sae firm aboot my memory they entwine.

Back to boyhood pranks an' plays, an' the woods o' nuts an' slaes
  Noo fond memory often lifts me in a dream,
An' this nicht I'm far awa', an' wi' bonnie Teenie Shaw
  Watch the lillies nodding at us frae the stream.

Oh, sic ranting times we had, helter-skelter lass an' lad,
  An' twa happier bairns on earth ye couldna see,
For I'd weave a rashy croon, then wi' daisies deck her roun',
  An' dream when grown a man my wife she'd be.
An' I mind, as 'twere yestreen, hoo the mirth danc'd in her een,
  While the sunlicht through her rippling locks did gleam,
As we hand in hand would gae, an' frae aff the Breckan Brae
  Watch'd the lillies nodding at us frae the stream.

Back to boyhood pranks an' plays, &c.

Noo for thirty years she's lain underneath the kirkyard
stane,
  An' my memory's speeding back through mist o' tears
Owre the graves that lie between, an' this nicht wi' her I've
been,
  While Time turns his dial back for forty years.
An' I'm hirpling doon life's brae, it will sune be gloaming
grey,
  The mune keeks owre the hills, the stars now gleam ;
But I still maun daunner back wi' my ghosts o' youth to
talk
  Where the lillies still keep nodding frae the stream.

    Back to boyhood pranks an' plays, &c.

"Daddy's Wee Boy."

I WOKE frae a dream between waking and sleeping,
When gray beams o' morn through the window were
peeping
For I found clasping airms roun' my neck fondly twine,
An' warm, rosy lips firmly prest against mine,
While my bonnie wee bairnie crept closely to me,
Wi' sic fun lauching oot o' his bricht hazel e'e,
An' he said wi' a sweet voice juist brimfu' o' joy—
"Oh! Da-da, dae ye like me?—I'm Daddy's Wee Boy."

Dae I like ye, my bairn?—ay, I like ye fu' weel,
An' ye'll ne'er ken, wee lad, a' the love that I feel,
But I pray through life's bruilzie, its strife, an' its steer,
May God guide in safety the feet o' my dear.
Though my bairn's only three, he's a bairn amang ten,
And maun sune carve his place amang big, muckle men;
But whate'er Time may bring, an' whate'er yer employ,
May it bring Faith and Wisdom to "Daddy's Wee Boy."

Ye'll hae sair howes to travel, an' dreich braes to speel,
But be manly through't a', an' ye're sure to dae weel;
An' though life's road seem dreary an' weary an' lang,
Let us fill it wi' love, an' then cheer it wi' sang;
An' I'd swap a' the fame that my puir muse could earn,
For the saft faulding airms an' the kiss o' my bairn;
May "Our Father in Heaven," that land o' pure joy
Keep a wee corner in it for "Daddy's Wee Boy."

Dreaming Alone.

HALF the years of our life in a dream-dance glide on,
    And the fond hopes we cherish grow bright
        bubbles blown ;
    Here, while grey mists creep round and the winds
        sob and moan,
    In the calm twilight hour I sit dreaming alone.
I am dreaming of dear ones that wander'd astray
Into bye-paths of sin—who fell dead by the way,
And of fair forms that rest 'neath their sad burial-stone,
In the hush of the twilight I'm dreaming alone.

Fondly dreaming of boyhood—its pranks and its plays—
And of rose-tinted hours spent in love's flowery maze ;
Of the chances we missed, of the lost, might-have-been ;
Of the hopes and despairs, and the graves strewn between
The fresh springtide of youth and the grey hairs of age ;
Of the haps and mishaps, and the blots on life's page,
And if some one will miss me and mourn me when gone ;
And thus dream crowds on dream while I'm dreaming alone.

To a Friend.

The gentleman to whom these lines were addressed, Mr. O. H.
Peck, holds a most responsible position in "The Marvellous
City of the Plains," as it has been called. In a letter he said,
"At our silver wedding we received a great many letters and
some poetical epistles, but your beautiful and well-written
poem was pronounced superior to them all." Mr. Peck also
enclosed the following extract from a letter written by Mr. B.
P. Shillaber, an eminent journalist and *littérateur*, and author
of the famous "Mrs. Partington" sayings, to whom copies of
some poems by Mr. and Mrs. Hyslop had been sent :—

"The poems you sent me are excellent all ; but the 'Sang of Hope' is as good
as anything Burns ever wrote. I can almost say better, for Burns in a serious
mood seems out of his element, while this breathes a most devout spirit. The
"Drifting" poem is likewise great. I like the lady's verses also. They show a
tender, womanly feeling. The Scotch dialect I often try, and tolerably well, so
they say. It is a dialect that "amaist sings itsel'," and I dearly love its musical
ring. If you have a copy of that "Sang of Hope" please send me one. It clings
about my memory like a painted thing."

MY swift thoughts take the wings of the morning,
    And the fleet, nimble feet of the roe,
Now o'er long leagues of land and of ocean,
    Like a whirlwind careering, they go ;
Where the long range of sentinel Sierras
    Stand hooded and bearded with snow,
Watching, through the long lapse of the ages
    Life's clamour and bustle below.

For where busy industry keeps stirring,
    Like hives of the ant or the bee,
To a spot near that glory of mountains
    The wings of my fancy will flee.
At the foot of these perilous passes
    Dwells one who hath grown unto me

Like a brother and friend, but whose features
    I never have seen, nor may see :
But whose pen, with its wonderful magic,
    Has talked, and keeps talking, with me.

Few and faint are the words I have spoken,
    In a feeble and faltering way,
Yet my thought met the soul of a brother,
    At the foot of these mountains astray.
Now each voice, through the darkness of distance,
    Is calling " Keep straight in the way
That leads on past the pits of Gehenna,
    To the light of the Infinite Day ;
We shall meet at the feet of our Father,
    In a fervour of worship for aye."

We have drank of the glory that rushes
    From the bright seraph down to the gnome ;
Though our lives may be toss'd by sin's tempest,
    Like feathers or flakes of the foam.
Here or there at the edge of the desert,
    Wherever our footsteps may roam,
We shall meet at the end of life's journey,
    When God calls his wanderers home.

They are holding their bright Silver Wedding,
    In Denver's young city to-night,
Though I sit with them there in the spirit,
    Yet a spirit has said to me " write ;"
But the thoughts through my brain that keep surging,
    My weak pen could never indite.

May their path to the gates of God's morning,
  Be peaceful, and radiant, and bright;
And the aureole grand of His blessing,
  Be round and about them to-night.

Though the firm earth like iron be clanking
  Where our feet touch a fringe of the snow,
Yet God's hand warms the roots of the daisies
  Till they dream of bright sunshine below.
Strike the rock with the wand of a Moses,
  And the clear living waters will flow;
So, in spite of the cold and the climate,
  Fond hearts in warm unison grow.

Here from this quiet nook in auld Scotland,
  From life's fierce bustle hidden away,
Two leal hearts this fresh wreath of good wishes
  On the lap of our friendship will lay.
While we lift up the voice of our spirits,
  And earnest and fervently pray:
" When life's fever of passions is ended,
  And your souls from their shells soar away,
May God hold thee and thine in His keeping
  For ever and ever, and aye !"

Wee Beenie.

AE day I gaed doon by yon burnie's side,
　　An' there, yoked wi' the Muses thrang,
Was lowsing the threads and thrums o' my thochts,
　　An' weavin' them into a sang;
Sae on, in a drowsy dream o' delicht,
　　I daunner'd the seggins amang.

When just at a bend o' the wimpling burn,
　　Through the faulds o' a leafy screen,
Amang bracken bowers, an' maist hid wi' flowers,
　　I spied oot a wee forest queen,
Wha sae shyly nodded, then lauch'd at me
　　Wi' her merry and twinkling een.

"Step owre to this side, wee wifie," I said,
　　"For richt fain wad I crack wi' thee;"
Sae, kilting her wee bits o' coaties up,
　　She sune rowed them abune her knee;
Then, wading across the braid brattling burn,
　　There cam' following after me
The bonniest, sweetest, wee bit lassie wean
　　That my auld een ever did see.

An' though blate at first, yet ere lang we strayed,
　　Wi' sae muckle o' mirth and fun,
To where broomy braesides lauch'd oot in flowers
　　To greet the warm fostering sun,
An' afore an hour had gaed owre oor heids
　　A' her heart I had fairly won.

For wi' cowslips sae sweet an' violets blue
  I sune twined for her a posie,
An' to save my life, oh ! I couldna help
  But cuddle her to my bosie,
An' to kiss her chubby, braw cheeks and chin
  An' her cherry lips sae rosy.

An' sae back an' forrit, an' oot an' in,
  We gaed roaming the wuds amang :
Until the sun had gane wastering doon
  We never ance thocht it was lang,
But listen'd an' heard the birds an' the bees
  Lilting owre the hale o' my sang.

Then gaed wi' her hame to her mither's door,
  Whaur the bracken laughs twist and turn,
Wha, wi' smiles and tears in her wat een said,
  " We thocht ye were droon'd in the burn ;
Oh, Beenie, sic grief to " dada " and " ma,"
  Had we haen oor wee bairn tae m'urn."

Awa wi' yer canting, ye thowless crew,
  Wi' cauld herts juist like lumps o' airn,
Wha wad miss the bliss that flows frae the kiss
  O' some blythe bit bonnie wee bairn ;
In yer fierce and grim race for cent.-per-cent.
  Ye ha'e still this grand truth to learn—

That ilk ane's a message sent straucht frae God,
  An' tells to the listening soul
That Love link'd wi' Beauty rules a' the warld,
  An' aye keeps it in firm control ;
An' His love sweeps upward frae flower to star,
  An' swift onward frae pole to pole.

Then here's to a' the bonnie laughing bairns,
    For, oh ! but I lo'e them rarely ;
Wi' their kisses sweet and their guileless words
    I trow they ha'e witch'd me fairly ;
An' my thochts flow oot in prayers to my God
    To bless them baith late and early.

A Glasgow Accident.

W' heids boo'd doon in Glasgow Toon sad hearts sit
    sabbing sair,
    An' list'ning for some weel-ken'd fit they'll hear on
    yirth nae mair ;
Ae sweep o' the Grim Reaper's scythe, wha dogs the heels
    o' Life,
An' mithers mourn their dochters, an' the husband mourns
    his wife.

The gurly day o' weet an' win' was drawing near its close,
When looder than the wailing win's a shriek of horror rose ;
Crushed deid amang their whirling wheels, nae tongue can
    ever tell
That rush for life, when owre their heids the strong walls
    reel'd an' fell.

The maids an' wives wha bore alike Life's warsle an' its
    load,
In health and strength last minute here, an' then the next
    wi' God.
In thocht I wi' the mourners sit, my muse wi' grief grows
    dumb :
I strive to speak some words o' cheer, but oh, they're dreich
    to come.

Oh, help wha can, nocht we can dae can fill ae lost ane's
    room ;
But oh, they nurse a double grief when hearts an' purse are
    toom.
Nane kens God's time ; sae let us leeve that, be it sune or
    lang,
Whene'er He sends His messenger we may be fit to gang.

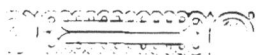

The Ending Year.

THE weeping year is sobbing to its end;
    Neighbour, what cheer?
What have we done, dear friends, to mar or mend
    Throughout the year?
Did we, while wandering over life's rough ways,
    Find some astray,
And lift, and up to higher levels raise,
    Then point The Way?
Pour'd balms of healing on each open scar?
    Spoke cheering words?
(Some words can cheer, while some cut deeper far
    Than two-edged swords)
Or, when some poor wretch, shiv'ring in the cold,
    For help did pray,
Pass, like the canting Pharisee of old,
    The other way?

Did we, when there was some sore wrong to right,
    Through praise or blame
Stand true and firm and faithful in the fight
    Till victory came?
The deeds we dreamed of at the last New-Year
    Are scarce begun,
And now in mists and frost its end draws near.
    What have we done?
How swift the years speed past us!   It doth seem
    But yesterday
Since this began, now like an ended dream
    Fading away.

How many haunting forms have passed beyond
     Our blame or praises ?
How sound they sleep, the faithful and the fond,
     Beneath the daisies.
Let us be brave and faithful at our posts ;
     Our pilgrim way
Leads on and up to join their wandering ghosts
     In endless day.

Soon swift as arrow speeding to its mark
     Death's dart will fall,
And from the glory hid behind the dark
     God's voice will call—
Fight the good fight ; be ready when you hear
     The passing bell,
Then go as to a feast and have no fear,
     For all is well.

The years into Eternity keep flowing,
Our good and evil deeds before us going ;
Be sure that we shall reap of our own sowing
     When we have done
With all the grieving and the sore deceiving
     Beneath the sun.
But till the number of our days be told,
     And we are here,
Let's welcome Christmas as we did of old,
     And glad New Year.

Sweet Wedding Bells.

Lines to His Grace the Duke of Portland, on his Wedding Day,
11th June, 1889.

ROLL and float out, sweet sound of wedding bells,
 A welcome to the bridegroom and the bride;
 Where'er the rich notes of your music swells,
  Tell to the listening people far and wide—
"Two souls to-day now join their fates together,
 And from this hour go forth hand linked in hand,
On to Life's duties and the great Forever
 Through the bright mazes of Love's flow'ry land."

Bring flute and viol, tread a heartsome measure,
 Let mirth and joy on every side abound,
And give this season to a round of pleasure,
 For we have now the open secret found.
That kindly deeds are grand and stronger far,
 Joined with the witchery of cheering words,
Than all the pomp and panoply of war,
 With roar of cannon and with flash of swords.

Not wealth alone makes happy ; we have known
 Some famous rich who in brave homes did dwell,
Whose presence seem'd as if a blast had blown
 Hot, fierce, and sulphurous from the pit of hell.
God loves the cheerful giver; from your store
 Your Grace did scatter where you saw the need;
Your sprig of promise grew, and evermore
 Did bud and blossom to some fruitful deed.

Some men make icicles of themselves with pride;
   You follow'd where the feet of Duty led,
You saw where want lay round on every side,
   Then clothed the naked and the poor were fed.
For deeds like these your honour'd name grew dear—
   True men like you become their country's pride;
For this the bells are pealing far and near—
   " God bless the bridegroom and his bonnie bride.'
And now round both on this your wedding day
   May God's best gifts and graces blend and meet,
And thus an humble bard presumes to lay
   His gift of verses at your Grace's feet.

Some Boyhood Memories.

Lines written for and Recited at the First Annual Re-Union of
Dumfriesshire Natives, held in Temperance Hall, Kilmarnock,
Friday Evening, 29th March, 1889.

GUID bless yer lauchin' een sae bricht,
　　I'm proud to meet ye a',
An' see sae mony here the nicht
　　At oor first gathering ca.'
Richt weel I ken'd ye wadna fail
　　To come frae near an' far—
Frae Nithsdale, Moffat, Annandale—
　　An' meddle us wha daur?

　　My birthplace in Glencairn—
Yet a' thae years can never blot
　　The memories o' the bairn;
An' that's the spell has drawn us here—
　　We're sweir and laith to tine
The memories that made life sae dear
　　In thae dead days langsyne.

When blythe as larks amang the cluds
　　We speil'd the breckan braes,
Or hied us to the hazel wuds
　　To gather nits or slaes;
At break o' day I've seen me oot—
　　A steerin', barefit bairn—
To pou' my lines or guddle trout
　　In either Nith or Cairn.

On Saturdays 'mang bent or seggs
   Ye'd foun' me without fail,
Thrang gathering gulls' or peaseweep eggs
   Abune "The Grey Mare's Tail ;"
Or sitting in "The Sutor's Seat,"
   I heard wi' deaving din
The broon burn's thund'ring doon in spate
   Owre bonnie "Crichope Linn."

Oh ! boyhood scenes, I mind them a',
   An' thocht whiles looking roon
Nae scenes sae braw as that I saw
   Frae tap o' "Tynron Doon."
Drumlanrig wuds and gardens fair,
   Hoo fresh ye come to min' ;
I've looked on scenes baith grand an' rare,
   But nane sae fair sinsyne.

Frae Cumnock to Glencaple Quay
   Nith speeds to meet the ocean :
A' doon its banks seemed juist to me
   A perfect " Land o' Goshen,"
Where plenty evermore did fill
   Her vales o' pastoral peace,
She slipt past Sanquhar an' Thornhill,
   An' on to fair Dumfries.

Dumfriesshire sons, through fire an' flame,
   In mony a Border Foray
Hae writ their names on scrolls o' fame
   An' in their country's story ;

An' twa o' these we haud maist dear,
    An' conjure with by turns—
Bruce leaning on his Carrick spear,
    An' minstrel Robert Burns.

In tomb an emperor micht hae plan'd
    The Poet's banes rest, where
As to a shrine from every land
    Do pilgrim feet repair;
On lands that own'd for mile on mile
    By Johnstones or Buccleuch;
We Irving bred an' Tom Carlyle,
    An' Joseph Thomson, too.

To "Surfaceman" that sings sae sweet
    Lark-sangs maist hauf divine,
I bend, an' lay doon at his feet
    This simple sang o' mine.
In memory o' ae happy time
    We spent wi' ane anither,
When wi' mad jokes an' swappit rhyme
    We en'd the crack thegither.

Hoo aft I've wish'd that I ance mair
    Fair Maxwelltown Braes could see,
Where I, wi' boy's heart free o' care,
    Gaed wammerin' like a bee;
To roam ance mair the auld craw wuds
    Or speil the breckan braes,
An' hear the laverock in the cluds
    Sing sangs o' ither days.

But tears wad blin' my een wi' rouk —
  The auld frien's a' are gane,
An' I wad walk 'mang fremit fowk
  A stranger and alane.
No ! better in my heart still keep
  The memories o' the bairn ;
But till Death rocks me soun' asleep,
  I'll no' forget Glencairn.

Noo, brethren a', I'll say " Guid nicht,"
  An' wish afore I gang—
" May a' yer lives be fair and bricht,
  And merry as a sang ;
And health and walth o' milk and meal
  To a' that's sitting here,
An' grant God keep ye hale and weel
  To meet anither year."

"That's My Bairn's Faither Noo."

IT was ae blashy winter nicht,
  When sleety cauld winds blew,
Some ane cam' up to me an' said,
  "That's my bairn's faither noo !"
I wonnert muckle what he meant,
  Wi' sic a care-worn broo,
When he cam' sichin' i' my lug,
  "That's my bairn's faither noo !"

For many a year I'd kent him as
  A doited, drouthy chiel,
Ane wha had lost a' guid, langsyne,
  In pleasure's dizzy reel.
"Weel, Tam, what's i' the win' the nicht ?"
  "Man, our wee Annie's deid,"
He said wi' mournfu' tone, an' shook
  His towsie, tawted heid.

"It's but ae nicht an' day since she
  Was playing with the lave,
An' ere twa days gang by we're gaun
  To lay her in her grave ;
An' see the auld grave-howker there
  (Mind what I tell ye's true),
Gangs inly kecklin' to himsel',
  "That's my bairn's faither noo !"

"Come, dinna droop, cheer up !" I said
  "Gin a' we're tell't be true,
She's maybe in a better warld,
  Among the angels noo."

"I dinna doot, I dinna doot,
   A word ye say ava,
But oh! *He* michna just hae taen
   Our bairn sae sune awa.

"For in our house twa years she made
   A simmer a' aroun',
But Death has steppet in the nicht
   An' fell'd the wee thing doon!"
"It's sin tae yammer; ills are aft
   But blessings in disguise,
An' this may be God's lowe o' love
   To licht you tae the skies!

"Gang hame, an' owre wee Annie's corpse
   Lean out your soul, to hear
The harpings for a new-made star,
   Up i' the heavenly sphere!"
"Guid-nicht!" he said, "I'll mind your words,
   An' use them if I can,"
Then shook my hand, an' walked awa,
   I hope a better man.

An' this was he I thocht had left
   A' guid, till it left him;
Noo, when grief probed love's hidden spring
   It bubbled to the brim.
Oh! may the great high power wha keeps
   A' nature in His care,
Breathe on puir Tam the breath o' life,
   An' bless him evermair!

What the Daisies Said.

THE daisies—modest, sweet, an' pure—
When gloamin' shadows fa',
　Steek up their e'en an' droop their heids,
　　An' dream the nicht awa';
But when the licht keeks through the lift—
　The reign o' darkness done,
　We see them lift their heids ance mair,
　　An' opening to the sun.

Sae, though misfortune's blasts may whiles
　Aroon' us dourly blaw,
We daurna mope, an' whinge, an' greet
　Amang its frost and snaw;
By cooring in the caves of grief
　Soul-murder may be done;
Up, an' look up, my hopeless frien',
　For that way lies the sun.

The hero-saints, we praise and bless
　Through a' oor Christian lands,
Ne'er won their croon wi' heids boo'd doon,
　Nor yet wi' faulded hands,
But firm, erect in self-respect,
　They press'd on in the van,
An' prov'd hoo firm oor God can build
　The Christ within the man.

His rich rewards to faithful souls,
　Long as the heavens endure,
To those who through this pilgrim land
　Walk strong, an' firm, an' pure,

An' strive to track the steps o' Ane
    Wha ance went on before ;
See yonder where His glory streams
    Through Heaven's open door !

An' if we mak' His law o' love
    Oor buckler an' oor shield,
When staggerin' feet through caves o' death
    To hills o' God ha'e spiel'd,
Then, like the pure, wee daisy flower—
    Life's nicht o' trials done—
Our souls shall lift their voice to praise
    The everlasting Sun.

Sae Wearie.

"WHAT means a' this rinning?
  It sets my heid spinning,
An' sair fankles the thochts in my brain;
  Through this riot an' routing,
  The steer and the shouting,
My sad heart just keeps sabbing wi' pain.

  An' oh! what mean thae bells?
  For their lood clanging knells
Aye gang "ding dong, ding dong" through my heid.
  Is't for bridal or birth?
  Do they jingle in mirth?
Or keep tolling a dirge for the deid?

  But they chanted nae dirge
  Owre the white heaving surge,
When the guid ship drapt doon in the sea,
  Whaur my man, rock'd asleep
  In some cave o' the deep,
Lies close hidden for ever frae me.

  Yet a' things look'd sae bricht
  When she passed frae oor sicht
Wi' the dear anes we a' lo'ed sae fain;
  But the guid "Aberdare"
  Frae that day nevermair
Was it seen on the waters again.

  Noo, for lang weary years
  O' strange hopes and sad tears
In vain quest went my soul on its track,

Till the years ha'e grown ten,
An' the boys ha'e grown men,
But the lost ones they never cam' back.

Though I strive at my wheel
Whiles to spin or to reel,
I'm juist waiting the signal to gang
Whaur the weary ha'e rest—
In the land o' the blest—
An' the dirge will break into the sang.

Aye, I wait for His ca',
An' will sune be awa'
Frae life's bustle, its strife, an' it's din ;
My guidman's on afore,
An' through yon open door
There will neither gang sorrow nor sin.

Noo, dear bairns, lay me doon,
An', oh, freen's, gather roon :
Hear that moan that comes up frae the sea,
Roon the ribs o' the coast
Creeps a desolate ghost
That keeps calling and beck'ning for me.

See ! the lang nicht's gane past—
It is morning at last,
An' the angels their sangs ha'e begun."
Then, in sicht o' them a',
She juist faded awa'—
Like a star in the licht o' the sun.

In God's Acre o' graves,
An' in sicht o' the waves,
Freen's, in tears, laid her under the sod ;
Though they toll'd no death-bell,
Yet they knew all was well
Where she dwelt—in the Kingdom o' God.

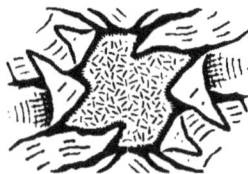

On a Wedding.

OH "rub-a-dub-a-dub," now the drums do play,
Stand back good people and clear the way,
For here comes the bridegroom, and his blushing
bride
Like a drooping lily now clings to his side.
Beating heart to heart, and thus hand in hand,
They pass on to the light of their rainbow'd land ;
'Mid a shower of rice and of laughter bright,
While "luck slippers" follow them in their flight;
For weal or for woe, from her father's door,
They now seek what the future may hold in store—
Then " rub-a-dub-a-dub," and beat the drum,
Joy, grief, and grey hairs with the years will come.

Now " tan-tan-tan-ta-raw " the trumpets blare,
And a volley of " welcomes " fill the air,
" God bless the bridegroom and his bonnie bride,"
Like incense floats round them from either side ;
And his manifold blessings around may fall
In a shower of good upon one and all ;
Now with loud " huzza's " they are whirl'd away,
On the bright sweet flight of their wedding day—
So "rub-a-dub-a-dub " now, and beat the drum,
But weal and woe with the years will come.

Then " tum-a-tum-a-dum," and tweedle-deedle-dee,"
On the wings of Joy let the moments flee ;
For though from our sight now the " young folks "
have flown,
Let the supper and mirth of the feast speed on ;

Strange hands will clasp in the dance to-night,
Will, ere long, in sweet wedlock's bonds unite ;
For, from Time's first hour till his latest day,
Fond youth and folly will have their way.
And while ages pass, and the earth spins round,
Men will hear some wedding bell's sweet sound ;
And the viol and trump and throbbing drum
Will make mirth for the weal and woe to come.

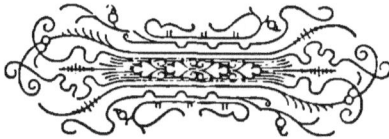

Guid Bless the Bairns.

AE day doon by the burnie's side,
　Yoked wi' the muses thrang,
I strove to catch my fluttering thochts
　An' weave them in a sang,
Sae in a maze o' sweet delight
　Gaed daunnering alang,

When juist across the wimpling burn,
　Hid by a leafy screen,
I spied a dainty little maid—
　A bonnie forest queen,
Wha shyly nodded owre to me
　Wi' lauchin' twinkling een.

"Step owre across, my sweet wee lass,
　For I fain wad crack wi' thee,"
Sae she kilted up her petticoaties
　Heich aboon her knee,
An' wadeing owre the brattling burn
　She followed after me,
The bonniest we bit lassikie
　My een did ever see.

Though blate at first, yet sune we stray'd,
　Wi' muckle mirth an' fun,
To where a brae laugh'd oot in floo'rs
　To greet the fostering sun,
An' ere an hour pass'd owre oor heids
　Her hale heart I had won.
F

For wi' cowslips an' wi' violets blue
   I twined for her a posie,
An' for my life I culdna help
   But cuddle her to my bosie,
An kiss her chubby cheeks an' chin,
   An' cherry lips sae rosie.

An', back an' forrit, oot an' in,
   We roved the wuds amang,
Until the Sun gaed wastering doon—
   We never thocht it lang,
But listen'd to the birds an' bees,
   For they had stown my sang.

'Mid sic a scene nae man could sing
   That " man was made to mourn."
We daunnert hame ; her mither said,
   " Ye've gi'en me sic a turn ;
O Beenie, bairn, I thocht ye droon'd
   In some weil o' the burn."

Awa', ye thowless, canting crew,
   Wi' hearts like lumps o' airn,
Ye miss the bliss flows frae the kiss
   O' some bit bonnie bairn ;
In your grim race for cent.-per-cent.
   Ye've still this truth to learn ;

Ilk ane's a message straught frae God,
   An' tells the listening soul
That love and beauty rules the world,
   And keeps it in control ;
An' His love flows from flower to star,
   An' on frae pole to pole.

Then here's to a' the bonnie bairns,
    For, oh ! I lo'e them rarely ;
Their kisses sweet and guileless words
    I trow ha'e 'witched me fairly,
An' my thochts flow oot in prayers to God
    To bless them late and early.

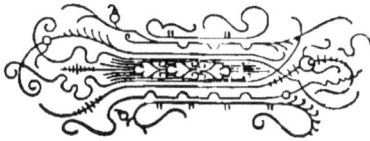

A Handful of Leaves.

Lines on receiving a bunch of dried leaves enclosed in a letter from
America.

FROM the grand old American forests
These crisp leaves—so rustling and sere—
Have come fluttering across the Atlantic
Unto me at the end of the year.
They are fill'd with the grand tints of sunsets
From Autumn's rare mellowing eves,
Though the voice of dull scoffer keeps saying,
"They are only a handful of leaves."

But the humming-birds through them went gliding
Like bees the bright blossoms among;
With odours and balm they are laden,
And an anthem of marvellous song.
We will lift them and lay them past fondly
With other things treasured and rare—
With a dear dead friend's last loving letter,
And our mother's soft, silvery hair.

If the dear one who sends us this token
Of the year and the season's decline,
Were but with us to-night in Auld Scotland,
We would pledge in a beaker of wine,
To the memory of hours that departed
In the dear, happy days o' langsyne—
If he only were with us in Scotland,
His fond hand claspt firmly in mine.

Since that bleak, dreary night in September,
 When we stood at the parting of ways,
My thoughts have kept following you ever,
 And will till the end of my days.
You left fond hearts behind you in Scotland,
 Who stretch hands to you over the sea,
And now send you their Christmas greetings,
 Best wishes and blessings to thee.

May your path aye be onward and upward
 In your quest after fortune or fame,
And we yet, ere the years be much older,
 May meet in the auld hoose at hame ;
But till that time we oft in the gloaming
 Will turn from the sorrow that grieves,
And take down our album of treasures
 To look at your handful of leaves.

Doleros.

CRUEL bird! from your eyrie's height
  Peering so fierce through the twilight grey
With a hungry look in your hungry eyes;
  Have your ravenous brood been fed to-day?

For darkness is falling o'er all the land,
  And hiding the sweep of the tumbling sea,
Your screams sweep past on the rising blast;
  Now what you are dreaming of, tell to me.

" Of the gurgling screams in a drowning ship,
  That dropt down fathoms deep as it neared the bay—
Of the corses will roll on the sobbing shore,
  With my beak in their hearts at the dawn of day."

" Oh, my heart sinks down with that sinking ship,
  For my lover speeds homeward across the sea
With wealth of gold from the far-off lands;
  He is coming to make a bride of me."

But the bird scream'd out, "See! your bridegroom comes!
  From the waves he is rising about your feet;
Lean down, lift him up as a gift from me,
  Though his bridal robe be a winding sheet."

*   *   *   *   *   *

They sought her down by the wreck-strewn beach
  At break of morn, and they found her there,
With her lover lock'd in her clasping arms,
  And the long sea-tangle among their hair.

To a Lady on her Wedding Day.

I CANNOT bring to grace your bridal board
    Rich gift of trinkets, but can only pray
God's dower of blessings on your dainty head,
    May His strong arm be round you night and day.

Not wealth but comfort do I wish for thee;
    For wealth needs care to keep, and may take wings,
In thriftless hands it proves a demon's curse,
    A Hydra-headed fiend that tears and stings.

May he who bears you to his quiet home,
    To fold you there his bosom's nestling dove
Find, while your hair grows grey through lapse of years,
    New gifts and graces with increase of love.

Bear and forbear. There lives no perfect thing
    In all this pilgrim land we wander through;
Let not ambition lure you in its tracks,
    Keep your tastes simple and your wants but few.

May both learn meekly at the Master's feet,
    Till life's light over, with its work well done;
God calls you to His mansions of the blest,
    In that bright land which is " an heavenly " one.

Hail! and farewell, now as you hither go,
    May God on both His choicest blissings pour;
And guide and guard you through the coming years,
    I cannot wish you less, nor wish you more,

The King has Called Me.

THE King has called me to His home to-night;
　Bring me white garments—raiment pure as snow,
For all things must be clean within, without,
　When I into His presence-chamber go
　To praise His name who now has stooped so low.

Two shining ones but now his message brought
　Here to this lower room wherein I dwell,
And, while their glory flooded all the place,
　They said, in tones clear as a silver bell,
　"The Master calls for you, and all is well."

I hear the music in the upper rooms;
　My soul like pent bird panteth to be free.
When that has pass'd beyond life's prisoning bars,
　Then burn, or bury—do what pleaseth thee—
　With the worn cage that is no longer me,
　For I shall neither know, nor hear, nor see.

O'er the cold clod where for a space I dwelt
　No loud lamentings make, nor sob, nor groan,
No useless flood of tears, nor vain regrets,
　Nor wringing hands for me when I am gone.
Through death's dark vale and up the golden stair,
　Christ's hand in mine—I go not forth alone,
　But go to meet the King upon His throne.

Sometimes, perchance, amid the hurrying years,
  With friends in shady nook or wooded glen,
You'll say, " He coined his soul's best thoughts in words,
  And sent them rushing through his ready pen
  In song of hope to cheer his fellowmen."

If any song of all the songs I've sung
  Makes any music where life's discord mars
God's harmonies, and through the souls of men
  Goes echoing on to heal some hidden scars,
  Then I shall hear it from beyond the stars.

"Peace on Earth, to Men Goodwill."

WHAT dream and vision of delight
   Broke on these watching shepherds' sight,
   When angel's straight before their eyes
Flung wide the gates of Paradise,
And thence on broad far-sweeping wings
God's message of salvation brings !
Praise God, in His redemption plan,
His Son became the Son of Man,
This day born in a low disguise,
At Bethlehem in a manger lies,
Whom men will doom to death abhorr'd—
The Saviour who is Christ the Lord :
" Peace be on earth, to men goodwill."
That angel song keeps echoing still.

Ring, Christmas bells, to high and low,
That message from the long ago ;
Ring out all ills, all good ring in
To haunts of want, of woe, and sin ;
Ring out the reign of evil deeds,
Ring in the fuseing of the Creeds,
Till every land and every tongue
Have learn'd the song the angels sung—
Till one grand psalm shall throb and thrill
From earth's far ends to Zion's Hill,
Of " Peace on earth, to men goodwill."

The Dream of a Masque.

PURSUIVANT—
      " Place for the Marshall of the Masque."

   CITIZEN—
" What thinkest thou of this quaint Masque?
   What thinkest thou of this quaint show of ours my
      friend?
   Even now we see the redness of the torches,
   And the clarions sound floating hither, round
   The pageant grows on the enchanted air;
   And see—see how the crowd divide
   Like waves before an admiral's prow."

A MARSHALMAN—
      "Give place to the Marshall of the Masque."
            Adapted from Shelley's Dramatic Fragments.

SLOW, with low hushing steps to my truth-seeking soul,
   One night a bright Presence came, aweing me dumb;
And out of the glory that zoned it, there stole
   The sound of a whisper that said to me, "Come."
And as one tied and chain'd to a wild dream of night,
   Speeds on through a maze of bewildering change;
So sped we, where grew to my marvelling sight,
   A weird, witching vision, most wonderful strange.

For somehow, my senses would say that I dream'd,
   And fancy was weaving her web unto me;
Yet all things more real and more tangible seem'd,
   Than a dream woven out of a fancy could be,

And first, then, methought we went groping our way
　　On through foul vapours dank, that kept clogging my
　　　breath,
Where in wreck and in ruin, all things round me lay
　　Muffled up in the long hushing silence of death.

Where the ivy, the nettle, and hemlock so rank,
　　Twisting thick with the moss round the burial-stones,
'Mid the drear desolation throve bravely and drank
　　Their life from the sap of the mouldering bones.
Strange, foul, loathsome reptiles were crawling, or lay
　　'Mid their ooze and their slime thro' the slumberous hours
Where for ages Time's tooth had been munching away
　　At the glory and pride of grand temples and towers.

And kinging this realm sat some horrible THING,
　　Its form or proportions I cannot declare,
　　For, ere I could note them, Fear backward did fling
　　The blood to my heart, and had stiffen'd my hair;
And I clung to my guide for some comforting cheer,
　　Yet no word did he speak, but kept pointing afar,
Where on sight's farthest verge a bright speck did appear,
　　Speeding down where we stood like a swift-falling star.

And he lifted me up, till from where we did stand
　　I saw as it near'd 'twas a fair land like ours,
With vales, rivers, seas, and tall mountains so grand,
　　Its woods filled with music, its gardens with flowers.
And I saw where the tide of souls ever did run,
　　Stirr'd by breezes of passion, with ebb and with flow;
And this fair, fruitful world seem'd woven in one
　　With that land in its shroud of hoar ruin below,

And the nations were there, of all colours and tongues,
    With the show of their symbols, their creeds, and their
        schools,
Who, with shouting strange follies kept spliting their lungs,
    Till the whole land seem'd fill'd with a racket of fools.
For each blew some bubble and call'd it by name,
    And in his heart's worship did place it for God,
And, mad in pursuit of Gold, Honour, or Fame,
    In a wild-heaving tumult down Time's dusty road.

Rob'd and masqued for their part thick the people did come.
    And louder and wilder the mad clamour swells,
To the tones of the organ, rub-dub of the drum,
    The thunder of cannon, and jangle of bells.
And on, on came that riot of wild madd'ning mirth ;
    On, on, ever on, without breaking or pause,
Where to me the rock-ribs of the flower-spangled earth
    Seem'd thin as a network of gossamer gauze.

But ever as on like fierce madmen they prest,
    I saw as they danced down life's treacherous ways,
That the circles were thinn'd, and some poor fools had rest,
    For lo ! they had danced to the end of their days.
And aye as kept dropping some gay dancing form
    Down to death's gloomy realm that low under did lie,
As up through the hush and the pause of a storm
    Comes the low muffled shriek of some drowning one's cry.

I heard, or my fancy said to me I heard,
    A sound like the rattle and clatter of bone,
As if the long dead in their coffins had stirr'd
    With a low, hollow, drear, and monotonous moan.

Still the wild madd'ning chase swept through sunshine and
    shade,
  As each circle danced to its own folly's tune,
And sick'ning and sad were the scenes that were play'd
  'Neath the bright staring sun and meek pitying moon.

But the loud voice of THE HORROR came floating to me
  From beneath, through, and over their thundering din,
'Fools and knaves, ye may dance with your caste and
    degree
Through your strange maniac circles of folly and sin ;
For I dance in the midst of each wild whirling ring,
  Let the measure you tread too, be slow or be fast,
Still the beggar in rags, or the proud crownèd king
  Creepeth down like lashed hounds to my regions at last.

"Chase your bubbles and dreams to their end and their
    doom,
  Through your Babel of noise, with your bustle and strife,
Yet ye all must grope out through my caverns of gloom
  Ere ye pass to the gates of the City of Life."
Slow the strange vision vanished, and left me alone,
  And my soul for its meaning still gropeth for light,
Till my years to the years of dead ages have flown,
  And Eternity reads me the weird riddle right.

    Oh ! 'tis a sad and weary world,
      This old one we are creeping through ;
    But years they come, and years they go,
      And soon the Old will be the New ;

The birthday of the newer life,
 An end to earth's tumultuous jars ;
The balm and calm of peace and rest,
 When death shall burst the bonds and bars

That hide the beauty and the bliss,
 And glory of the golden prime,
When God shall walk with sons of men
 As in the world's young Eden time.

And *somewhere* past yon jagged peaks
 The surges dash against the shore
Whose hungry tongues shall lick us off
 Into the endless evermore.

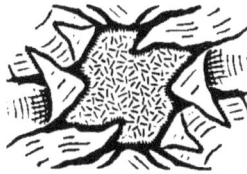

Fever-Stricken.

DEEP the dreary winter folded town and hamlet,
wood and wold,
   In a web of frozen snow-flakes till they dream'd
amid the cold
Of the coming spring-time's glory, of the beauty that would
be,
When the south-wind kiss'd to blushing, hilly slope and
sunny lea.
Then a fever caught and chain'd me moaning on my bed of
pain,
With a breath of Etna blowing, scorching up my blood and
brain,
Till I sigh'd for cooling snowdrifts, with a river at my lips,
And the world around grew darken'd in a strange and
drear eclipse.

Then my barque of life went drifting out into a tumbling
sea,
Where the stormiest winds of heav'n beat and buffeted at
me ;
With no guide, nor chart, nor compass, in deep waters all
alone—
By the breath of fierce tornadoes, like a feather I was blown ;
Then a calm came, and some angel, pitying, gazed into my
face
For a moment, till the tempest drove me from my halting
place,
And the storm-fiends and the demons from the caverns
where they dwell,
Clutch'd and suck'd me through some malestrom down the
sulph'rous jaws of hell.

Swift the scene changed : Now I wander'd in some old
cathedral town,
Black with smoke and dust of ages through the centuries
looking down ;
Long since, from this ancient city, life and strength had
taken wings,
And the spider webs were rotting in the palaces of kings.
Nought disturbed the awful silence, save my footfalls
stumbling on ;
Ghosts of dwellers long since moulder'd underneath their
burial-stone,
Watch'd me in the deep'ning twilight search for what I
could not find :
Webs of darkness hung before me, thicker darkness lay
behind.

Cold and bleak the night was falling when this marvel I did
see,
All the quaint house-tops were bending slowly down to
cover me,
While my hair with horror stiffen'd, and I strove to leave
the place—
Like a smile flash'd out from Heav'n came once more the
haunting face—
Came and left me vainly cleaving denser darkness than
before,
Like a soul that pants for pardon, hurled back from Eden's
door :
Then strange voices groan'd and mutter'd through the thick
and lurid gloom,
And the city reel'd and stagger'd, crumbling in its crash of
doom.

Next 'mid floods of blinding sunshine, somewhere in the
    torrid zone,
Through dense jungles, dread Saharas, I was madly speeding
    on,
For behind I heard the howling of a fierce and hungry
    pack
Of tawny lions, speckled tigers, bounding down upon my
    track,
While the sharp spears of the Cactus tore the flesh from off
    my bones,
Snakes and lizards hiss'd and wheetl'd at me from their
    hiding stones ;
Then I felt, when foil'd and beaten in this weird and fearful
    race,
That the arms of love were round me, and I knew my
    mother's face.

Slowly back to health I rallied from these weeks of fever-
    pain,
But its horrid scenes and visions burn'd themselves into my
    brain,
And will haunt the halls of mem'ry till I mingle with the
    dead,
And these eyes are closed for ever underneath the coffin-lid.
Noise of storms and crumbling cities, and that wild and
    awful race,
When the meek and pitying angel took my own dear
    mother's face,
Past life's later scenes of pleasure, rainbow'd hopes, and
    mist of tears,
They have come to-night to haunt me from their grave of
    twenty years.

The Wearie Weird.

MY faither cam' hame ae winter nicht
    Frae his daunnerin's through the toon,
An' slipt aff tae bed wi' an achin' heid,
    For the fever had fell'd him doon.

An' sae we sat doon tae oor lanely watch,
    My mither, my sister, an' I ;
For we fear'd frae the first he was grupt by death,
    An' the struggle wad sune be by.

An' for ten lang days an' nichts he lay,
    Wi' a tossin' an' moanin' sair ;
Then his speerit sped oot thro' the mirk midnicht,
    Tae the endless Evermair.

There were nane but oorsels tae close his een,
    Nae ithers o' kith or o' kin ;
An' we couldna weel blame puir neebor-folk,
    Though nane o' them ventured in.

Sae my mither and sister they streekit him oot,
    An' wash'd him clean an' sweet ;
While I huddled awa' in a corner dark,
    An' lang an' sair did greet.

Not the flood o' tears that ease the pain,
    For my een were scorch'd an' dry ;
But the draps that row back on the heart like lead,
    Tae blister whaur they lie.

But lang ere the white deid-claes were made,
  He was stiff an' cauld as stane ;
An' we three wi' burstin' hearts began
  Tae dress the corpse oor lane.

An' ane o' us lifted his ice-cauld heid,
  An' the ither ane took his feet,
While oor mither, wi' her ain tremblin' hauns,
  Row'd him up in his winding-sheet.

Then we coorit us doon roun' his empty chair
  Beside oor sad hearth-stane,
Wi' a cry tae the Heevins tae guide us noo,
  Since the heid o' the hoose was gane.

But he hadna been lang happit up i' the mools,
  Till a dwaminess owre me fell,
An' I pined till I pined clean aff my feet,
  Then lay doon wi' the fever mysel'

I ha'e mind, as I lay wi' the rackin' pain,
  Ne'er steekin' the licht frae my een,
Some letters were brocht me tae my bedside,
  Frae a tried and trusted freen'.

Though he's waggin' his pow in a pu'pit noo.
  Wi "Reverend" tae his name,
An' I'm but a puir half-gangrel chiel,
  We're aye "Tom" an' "Jack" the same—

As when first we met, twa laddies baith,
   Preein' sweets frae the muses' rill ;
Near a score o' years ha'e row'd by since then,
   But the boy's love clings tae us still.

An' the brave, strong words o' cheer he sent
   Tae me then, did comfort me :
An' I hae the letters beside me yet,
   An' wull keep them till I dee.

Weel, for weeks, lang weeks, atween life an' death,
   I focht an' I warslet sair,
Till the Power abune, at his ain guid time,
   Raised me up tae my feet ance mair.

But I scarce had begun, through oor cheerless hoose
   Wi' a stick tae hirple roon',
When my mither an' sister, wi' watchins worn,
   Were baith this time laid doon.

Then a' fell on me, but a strength was gi'en
   That couldna be a' my ain,
For I crept through the hoose by nicht an' day,
   Jist a thing o' skin an' bane.

'Twas a black, a bitter, an' dreary time
   O' sad woe tae mine an' me ;
Oh, friens ! may siccan a spate o' grief
   Come never tae thine nor thee.

But tho' a' lour'd gloomy an' dark awhile,
　An' God's chast'ning airm was bared,
Yet ane by ane He lifted us up,
　An' the three o' us still are spared.

Oh, ye wha are lolling in wealth an' pride!
　What are sic-like scenes tae you? —
Do you ever dream o' the dreary fauchts
　That puir folk warsle through?

There are thoosands wad let want gnaw life oot,
　An' starve tae the skin an' bane;
But wadna boo low tae a purse-prood knave,
　Nor mak' a puir mouth tae ane.

But the crust frae the haun' o' the kindly puir,
　Wi' little eneuch far theirsels,
Weighs mair wi' God, than the rich man's cake
　That's gie'n wi' a jingle o' bells.

An' it's only the puir can pity the puir,
　An' tae us sic deeds were dune
In oor later need, they'll be written doon,
　In the buiks o' God abune.

There are some o' thae kindly hearts sin' syne
　Tae their rest i' the grave lain doon;
While we're creepin' ahint in the same dreich road,
　Till oor God's ain time comes roon'.

Ye'll say my tale's but a ravel't hasp,
    Baith fankled in tweel an' reel ;
But ye brawly see what I'm eetlin' at,
    An' ken what I mean fu' weel,—

That the mirkest hour in the mirkest nicht
    Stretches oot tae a bricht'ning dawn,
An' sorrow an' care are but means through which
    We nearer tae God are drawn.

'Twad be weel, as we wade through the wearie weirds
    We whiles through life maun dree,
Tae look up wi' faith's e'e through the loutin' cluds,
    An' the guidin' Hann' tae see.

It wad keep a psalm in oor hearts for aye,
    As we trudge through life alang :
Till the notes we begin tae croon here sae low,
    Break intae the angels' sang.

SONGS.

My Faither's Gun.

IN the hin' o' the hairst, at the shuitin' time,
  Ae day I resolved I wad ha'e some fun,
    Sae wi' pouther an' hail tae the muzzle did prime
My faither's queer antediluvian gun.
Noo for thirty years it had hung, an' mair,
  This blunderbuss rusty an' auld an' broon,
On a cleek in the spence below the stair,
  An' was ance i' the year for the craws ta'en doon.

      Chorus—
        Oh, some fowk are born under Fortune's smile
          An' to a' things pleasant beneath the sun,
        While here I'm dacing three months in jail
          For a wee bit ploy wi' my faither's gun.

A hare frae the whins started aff' like mad,
    I had lifted my gun an' maist let fly ;
"Just show me your license my canny lad,"
    Quo' the voice o' the Gauger riding bye.
" It's amang oor neeps, ye meddlesome cauf,
    An' it needs this doze o' pouther an' hail ; "
But ere ye cud wink the blamed thing bang'd aff,
    An' gaed pepp'ring about his auld meer's tail.

Chorus—
    Oh, some fowk are born, &c.

"Oh, catch him, he's riddled me noo !" he yell'd,
    Sae wi' fricht I took to my heels an' run,
For I thocht baith rider an' horse were fell'd,
    Wi' that shower o' hail frae "My faither's gun."
" I'm deein !" he grunted, wi' pech an' grane ;
    But while fast I fled from my gath'ring foes,
O'd my fit play'd stot on a muckle stane,
    An' cowpin' across I broke my nose.

Chorus—
    Oh, some fowk are born, &c.

" Look !" said the Bobby that took me in chairge,
    "Juist look at his wild an' his rolling e'e ;
He's a dangerous chap to be gaun at lairge,
    He'll get better kept quaite by himsel' a wee."
Sae wi' bluidy nose, an' in shame an' grief,
    Wi' the tag-rag roon me, in rank and file,
I was mairched three miles like a cadging thief,
    And then safely lodged in the County Jail.

Chorus—
    Oh, some fowk are born, &c.

When in coort at last, said the judge in wrath :
  " Three months, noo, my man, we hae fixed for thee !"
Sax weeks hae pass'd, noo I'm grown like a lath,
  Fed on thin soor dook and skillagolee.
Ye may tryst my hearse, but ae' boon I crave,
  When ye've happit me sax feet under the grun ;
Will some o' ye write abune my grave :
  " HE WAS KILL'D WI' A SHOT FRAE HIS FAITHER'S GUN !"

  Chorus—
  Oh, some fowk are born, &c.

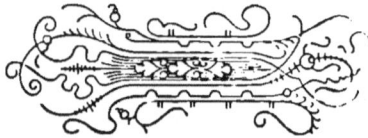

Keep Booing.

SANDY BAXTER, the Laird o' Whinbrae,
    Said, "Noo, frien', if ye ettle to spell,
An' to mak' ony mark in yer day,
    Ye maun juist ha'e a back like an eel.
Ye may lauch as ye like, honest man,
    But whatever pursuit yer pursuing,
O'd, ye'll fin' it's a sensible plan
    To keep smiling, an' becking, an' booing.

Chorus—

    It's a fact, if ye ettle to spell,
      An' no to dive heidlang to ruin,
    Ye maun juist ha'e a back like an eel,
      An' keep booing, ye sinner, keep booing.

Patie Gomeral, as a' bodie kens,
    Becks an' boos like thae slaverin' Turks;
Though his heid be as thin as a hen's
    Yet, guid faith, noo he's Maister o' Wurks.
An' hoo, think ye, this sumph o' a chiel
    Speil'd up to the heicht we're reviewing?
Weel, his back was as limp as an eel,
    Sae he raise to distinction by booing.

*Chorus—*It's a fact, &c.

There's oor dashing precentor, guid save us,
    Wi' the Saturday's " peat-reek " still grueing,
On the Sunday lilts psalms like a mavis,
    That the hale o' the kirk fowk's aloowing.

Though this rattling an' rollicking deil
  His ain paith to perdition keep's hewing,
O'd, his back can bob juist like an eel,
  An' he's gran, oh, he's gran' at the booing.

     Chorus—It's a fact, &c.

Frae the nobleman doon to the sweep,
  If ye look aroun', canny reviewing,
Ye will see hoo they wheedle an' creep,
  To some bigger buck becking an' booing ;
An' the man that will daur to stan' straucht,
  An' wi' scorn their mean conduct keeps viewing,
Will fin' life's but a wearisome faucht
  If he hisna' the gran' gift o' booing.

     Chorus—It's a fact, &c.

Willie's Waddin'.

"ROO, what's a' the steer an' the dirdum the day?
  For here hauf the hale kintra side seem
   paddin."
"Man, what dae they ca' ye, an' whaur cam' ye frae,
 When ye heard nae news o' wee Willie's waddin'?
For this thirty years he has leev'd—aye, an' mair,
 In his howf at the en' o' Hillhead loaning
A' his wearfu' lane, whaur the win's at night
 Wi' a sough like the Barrs of Ayr gang moaning.

Chorus—

 "Then fye let us a' gang to Willie's waddin',
  We'll be canty the nicht at Willie's waddin':
 If ye gang there ye'll see, atween you an' me,
  A rollicking spree up at Willie's waddin'.

"Willie's maist as thin as a speldrin' or slate,
 The feck o' his bouk's made o' broon skin an' bane:
While his bride frae the Raploch, big slav'ring Kate,
 Brings the weys wi' a dunt doon at fourteen stane.
An' the Laird o' M'Nab he has lent them his barn,
 An' wi' evergeen branches busk'd it brawly,
An' fowk frae the Carse crood to join in the farce
 Fae neuks in the hills to the en' o' the valley.

  Chorus—"Then fye, let us a'. &c.

"Sune Mess John speaks the words they're noo man an'
  wife,
 An' tied firm together for better or waur:
Weel they'll fecht, whiles then 'gree like you or like me,
 Sae deil tak' the hin'most, an' meddle wha daur.

" Fa' tae, fowk, fa' tae, there's a lot lads to dae ;
  Mak' yersel's a' at hame, juist tak' what ye please.
There's jelly in mugs an' yill in thae jugs,
  An bourock's o' bannocks and big whangs o' cheese.'

      Chorus — " Then fye, let us a', &c.

See, there's puddings in heaps, fried eels, partan taes,
  Haggis an' flounders, an' gran' ' Cookie-Leekie,'
An' doon frae a jeist, to help on wi' the feist,
  Hings a bletherfu' or twa o' rale Peat Reekie.
Then wi' pech an' stech, an' " Here's to ye " gaun roun,
  Drank each ither's toast in yill, whusky an' rum,
Till dazed een grew blear'd, an' the wutch cannels leer'd,
  An' kytes were hooved oot like the rim o' a drum.

      Chorus—" Then fye, let us a', &c.

While fiddlers play'd " diddle " up, back an' doon middle,
  An' fowk were slow through the Gran' March paraudin',
Wull an' Kate graip'd their weys to an' aul' hay laft,
  An' were rock'd asleep wi' " hooch's " o' the waddin'.
They were missed when cocks craw'd " Cockie-leerie-la,"
  Oot to seek the lost, fowk gaed staugh'rin an' wending,
But made beds here an' there at the back o' the dykes,
  Sae this brocht the spree to a sudden ending.

The toozie-boozie spree up at Willie's wadding
  O' the queer clanjamphrey at Willie's wadding ;
Ye'll keep min like me, till the day ye dee,
  O' the " omnium-gatherum " at Willie's wadding.

"We Wandered by the Dean."

TWAS when Spring had clad the wuds wi' her livery o
    green,
        Wi' airm aboot my lassie's waist I wander'd by
        the Dean,
Whaur twa brattling burnies mix'd in ae braid and
    deepening stream,
We wove oor lives thegither in the wab o' Love's young
    dream.
Though in the plantin close at haun' was heard the cushet's
    croon,
An' drousy hum o' noises cam' frae Killie's reeky toon,
We only watched the babes o' love dance in each ither's
    een,
Till mune an' stars keek't at us as we wander'd frae the
    Dean.

Again we walk'd—'twas Simmer, an' oor bairns were by
    oor side,
There didna beat mair happy hearts in a' the kintra wide,
The lark's sang 'mid the blinding blue was quivering
    through the air,
Like lambs oor wee tots frisk'd aboot as free o' guile an'
    care,
For they raced an' chas'd each ither, syne paidlin' to us
    cam',
Their daidlies filled wi' daises ower the Bonnet-maker's
    Dam,
Then pu'd the yellow cowslips 'mang the wuds and braes till
    e'en,
An' gloamin's plaidie hapt us as we wander'd frae the Dean.

Years after, when oor bairns had grown braw women an'
    brave men,
Ae son cam' doon frae London toon some holidays to
    spen',
An' prood to show his bairns the place whaur he sae aft
    had been,
Wi' blythe an' happy hearts ance mair we wander'd by the
    Dean.
The sun was sinking slowly doon among the rosy cluds,
The changing hues o' Autumn made a glory in the wuds,
Oor gran'-bairns frae the muckle toon thocht a' a fairy
    scene,
An' starry lamps were lichted when we wander'd frae the
    Dean.

Ance mair I wander by the Dean—nae joy it brings to me,
The cranreuch cauld o' Winter lies on ilka thing I see,
My hair, ance like the raven's wing, is white noo as the snaw,
My wife, my bairns, my early freens, hae a' been wede awa'
Sae lang I've grat owre heavy griefs, my tears hae a' ran
    dry,
But sune I'll meet owre yonder wi' my darlings by-an-bye,
Yet till death blaws oot the licht that noo flickers in my een,
I'll no forget the happy hours we wander'd by the Dean.

On March with "Pilgrim."

A SONG OF CHEER.

SAD neighbour, why moaning and grieving,
    With the gloom of the grave on your face?
Have you found love and friendship deceiving,
Have your idols been swept from their place?
Though you stand in this pitiful plight,
    With the cold world sneering and scorning;
Though your weeping endures for a night,
    Joy will come with the footsteps of morning.

Oh, look up!—foot it bravely and steady,
    For though grief saps your blood and your brain,
One has trod out the winepress already,
    We will drink at his fountain again.
Then onward, press onward, my brother,
    And still as we journey along,
We will tell o'er our joys to each other,
    And comfort our souls with a song.

See, we've pass'd through the Valley of Shadows;
    We have conquer'd old Giant Despair;
Here are cool waters skirting the meadows,
    Lambs bleat, and the roses are fair.
Now, all praise to life's bountiful Giver,
    We on Mountains Delectable stand;
See where over yon black, seething river
    Floats the White Christ with beckoning hand.

Soon the crest of death's wave of full blessing
  Will break on eternity's shore ;
We shall meet all our lost and our missing,
  When this life's well-fought warfare is o'er.
Let us on, then, dear sister and brother,
  And aye as we journey along
We will tell o'er our joys to each other,
  And comfort our souls with a song.

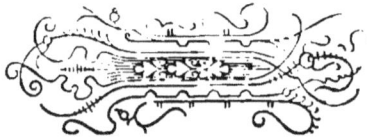

Scotland owre the Sea.

AN EMIGRANT'S SONG.

WHILE mirth an' fun keep bizzing thrang,
    An' joy rings through the ha',
  I fain would sing ae ither sang
    Before I leave ye a'.
'Tween this an' hame the saut sea rows,
  But thochts like swallows flee
To where blue bell an' heather grows,
  In Scotland owre the sea.

Chorus—Fill bumpers fou, an' there's my hand,
    We'll pledge this toast thegither :
      " Oor Scottish land, her mountains grand,
      Blue bonnets, kilt an' heather."

Fowk say we craw an' loodly blaw
  Oor ain wee tooting horn,
But foul befa' loons wad misca'
  The land where we were born.
She bred brave birkies in the past,
  She's dauntless still an' free,
An' oor best love lies anchor'd fast
  In Scotland owre the sea.

Chorus—Then "oor side yet," wi' heart an' hand, &c.

We sing her sangs wi' mirth an' tears,
  Oor haun graips for a sword

At thochts o' those through "killing years"
  Kept Cov'nant wi' the Lord.
We're "a' ae oo," ae mither's bairns,
  An' oh! ance mair to be
'Mang glens, lochs, bens, an' storied cairns
  In Scotland owre the sea.

Chorus—Noo ane an' a', link'd hand in hand, &c.

Bigging a Nest.

I HEARD twa birds talk to themsel's in the gloamin'
    Ere beneath their warm wings they had faulded
        their een,
As beside the Lang Wud wi' glad heart I gaed roaming
    To meet my braw lassie sae trig and sae clean.
The last keek o' daylicht was tintin the plantain,
    The sun was just sinking low doon in the west,
When I heard thae twa birds—wi' their bosoms pantin'—
    Sit chirping sae fain aboot biggin a nest.

" Noo listen ae minit, sweet Jenny my woman,
    The cauld winter blasts will be here afore lang ;
Blae-nebbit Jack Frost wi' dour fingers is coming
    To fauld up the threads an' the thrums o' oor sang.
Sae afore the days pass o' oor jinking and jouking,
    Dae ye no think, my bonnie wee bride, it were best,
While we've lang days an' sunshine we twa should gang
        looking
    For some cosie bield, an' there biggin' a nest ?"

Juist then my dear Maggie cam' smirkin' an' lauchin',
    An' a bonnier lassie my een never saw,
" Did ye hear what the birds said ?" quo' I, in my daffin',
    But she cuist doon her heid an' said naething ava',
" Noo, Maggie my darling, why hanker an' swither ?
    We've lo'ed ither lang, sae put love to the test,
Let us e'en buckle tae an' we twasome thegither
    Will sune big an' theek a bit cozie wee nest.

Maggie blush'd an' said: "John, for your sake I kept single,
  I micht been a leddy, sae bien an' sae braw,
But I ken when we sit roon oor ain cozie ingle
  The warm cloak o' love will be cleeding for twa."
Though its lang years sinsyne, whiles wi' bairns roon' us
    ranting,
  We watch the sun sinking low doon in the west,
An' tell o' that nicht, when beside the Lang Plantain,
  We heard the birds talk aboot bigging a nest.

Charley Chapman.

WEEL, juist twa verse,
  Ye hear I'm hearse,
An' canna sing a stave, man ;
    Or else I'd be
    Right glad to gie
A sang as weel's the lave, man ;
    An' if owre lang
    I mak' my sang,
Ye'll cry, for guidesake stap, man ;
    I'll dae my best,
    Ye'll dae the rest,
For sake o' Charley Chapman.

Chorus—

  Up frae yer seat
  An' fill up neat
O' barley bree a drap, man ;
  Then toast like me
  Wi' three times three,
"Success to Charley Chapman."

  Ye a' ken weel
  The sort o' chiel
We've come to honour here, man ;
  Staunch frien' in need,
  His word an' deed
Are kent baith far an' near, man.
    Baith nicht an' morn
    May Plenty's horn

Keep reaming owre the tap, man ;
Health an' lang life,
An' sune a wife,
We wish for Charley Chapman.

Chorus—

Up frae yer seat
An' fill up neat
O' barley bree a drap, man :
Then toast like me
Wi' three times three,
" Success to Charley Chapman."

Song.—"The Postman O'."

Y'VE pledged to mony a toast, an o' this an' that did boast :
    In ae reaming bumper mair, pledge "The Postman O'."
Amang a' oor working men, an' this truth richt weel ye ken,
    If there's ane we couldna spare, it's "The Postman O' ;"
For whaure'er he gangs are seen langing looks frae wistfu' een,
    That are watching ilka airt, for "The Postman O':"
While kind words, frae auld an' young, drap like honey frae the tongue,
    An' mak' sunshine in the heart o' "The Postman O'."

Chorus—Then a toast wi' three times three
    To "The Postman O',"
For wi' news owre land an' sea
    Comes "The Postman O' ;"
We would wait an' weary lang,
An' think a' things had gane wrang,
Did we miss the rat-a-tat
    O' "The Postman O'."

When the schule-weans chant an' sing, jouk and dance, at jingo-ring,
    Their clear voices blending sweet, spie "The Postman O' ;"
Some wee toddler frae the band rins to grup him by the hand,
    For wi' glee the bairnies' meet wi' "The Postman O'."

Wi' love lauching in her ee', for her lad's across the sea,
  Some lassie watches, weary, for "The Postman O';"
Sae the auld fowk's smirking smiles, an' the young ane's
    witching wiles,
  Aye mak' his wark sae cheery for "The Postman O'."

Chorus—Then a toast, &c.

There the feckless. auld, and puir, their lives barren as a
    muir,
  Are watching like their betters, for "The Postman O',"
For some dear anes far frae hame may be deid, or sunk in
    shame,
  In vain they look for letters frae "The Postman O'."
They wha leeve by deeds unfair, an' wad grup their
    neibour's share,
  Watch, as they wad watch a thief, for "The Postman
    O';"
While some wait freens coming back, but get letters edged
    wi' black;
May God guide them through their grief, sighs "The
    Postman O'."

Chorus—Then a toast, &c.

For he mak's us lauch sae glad, or he leaves us sabbing sad,
  News o' wadding, death, or birth, brings "The Postman
    O';"
Till we're laid amang the mools, an' are clappit doon wi'
    shools,
  We maun tak' baith grief an' mirth frae "The Postman
    O'."

Frae where fierce siroccos blow, an' owre Polar frost an'
    snow,
  Frae where Western wuds are fell'd comes "The Postman
    O';"
Frae the East, West, North, or South, frae where man or
    trade have growth,
  For the world's strong pulse is held by "The Postman
    O'."

    Chorus—Then a toast, &c.

"Oor Cookie Shine."

Post Office Annual Social Meeting, 17th Feby., 1888.

I'M a quate an' simple chiel, but I'm prood to see ye weel,
    An' sae mony smiling faces roon me here ;
Though my heid seems in a creel, an' keeps spinning like a wheel,
    'Od, oor meeting, frien's, comes only ance a year.
If fowk's happy, what's the odds ? Why sit glum like croaking toads,
    An' gang clinkum-clankum aye in chains an' fetters ?
Fill yer glasses, comrades mine, an' " Here's to oor Cookie Shine,
    An' this company o' Famous Men o' Letters."

There, each sonsie wife, 'od bless me, seems to whisper " Come an' kiss me,"
    An' the lassies too, guid bless the bonnie dears,
Their lauchin' een are dancin' in a wab o' love's romancing,
    That will brichten an' grow stronger wi' the years.
Though at Christmas an' New Year we had sic a bizz an' steer
    That oor heids an' backs were nearly dung agee,
Yet we're here noo safe at last frae the bustle an' the blast,
    An' we'll hae ae nicht o' fun, an' that ye'll see.

Min', I ne'er will praise the sot wad let a' things gang tae pot,
    Wad starve his bairns an' wife an' bruise an' kick her ;
I could tak' a whup mysel' and thrash them till they yell,
    That wad sae abuse the virtues of good liquor.

But a wee drap's unco guid, thaws the ice within the bluid,
  An' it lifts fowk up ayont the reach o' care ;
An' when boo'd wi' grief an' wrangs it will set them singing
    sangs,
  Sae what cuif wad grudge "a wee tot" for our share.
An' since here this nicht we're met juist a happy family set,
  Wi' sang, an' dance, an' fun we will keep the game afloat ;
"Here's a health to thee an' thine," pledge a toast to "me
    and mine,"
  May ne'er be waur amang us than "a wee drappie o't."

The Sang o' Hope.

WHEN stern misfortune clasps ye roun',
 Till faith seems gane wi' a' the lave,
An' a' life's joys wi' sods hapt doon,
Seem hid within some darling's grave.
Oh! ne'er sit doon to sab an' greet,
 Like owls in sunshine, blink an' mope,
Shake aff the mools—start to yer feet,
 An' listen to this sang o' hope—

   " Though driech to speel each dizzy heicht,
    And briery howes seem lang an' dreary,
   Frae caves o' nicht springs mornin's licht;
    Juist bide a wee an' dinna weary."

Though griefs may rive wi' mony a pang,
 Aye mind there's Ane that guideth a',
Keep heart o' grace, and He ere lang
 Will row the kirkyard stanes awa'.
See yon black cluds noo smoor the lift,
 Nor leave ae blink o' Heavin's blue;
But sune the darkness will be cleft,
 An' floods o' glory surging through,

For owre ayont yon snaw-clad hills,
 An' gruesome caves where shadows hide,
Are flowers, an' birds, an' streams, an' rills,
 An' sunshine on the ither side.
E'en when at last, wi' limpin' feet,
 Through death's dark vale o' fear ye grope,
Ye'll hear, come floating laigh and sweet,
 Frae hills o' God the sang o' hope—

"Though driech to speel each dizzy heicht,
 An' briery howes seem lang an' dreary,
Frae caves o' nicht springs mornin's licht ;
 Juist bide a wee an' dinna weary."

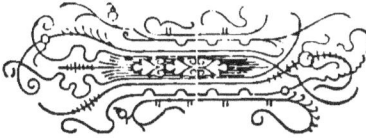

BALLADS.

Lady Maude's Tryste.

[While composing the following ballad, there was running in
my memory that sometime, somewhere, I had read a story, or
legend, in which the bride was described as having stabbed her new
wed husband—the union being against her wishes ; and that when
she was found by the wedding guests, she told them to "tak' up
yer bonnie bridegroom." Thus far and no further did memory
serve me at the time. About a fortnight after the verses were
written out, and while wondering where I could have read the legend,
there flashed at once on me the story of "The Bridal of Baldoon,"
which Scott has used to such good purpose in his "Bride of
Lammermoor." Considering it was at least 25 years since I had
read the novel, little wonder it had escaped my memory. There
was certainly no intention on my part to enter the lists with Sir
Walter. Only in one instance is there any similarity, while the
introductory scene and rounding up of my ballad are entirely
different. Even Sir Walter's version of the story, I am much afraid,
would not bear at this date the crucial test of strict investigation,
and would almost resolve itself into a myth, there being so many

versions of the story extant. In one of these it is the bridegroom who is stabbed, in another it is the bride; one will have it the effects of witchcraft—the bride being "harled out of bed by spirits and so maltreated that she died"—no word of stabbing here. In this ballad I have altered, and adapted to my own fancy, a tragic story which had made a strong impression on my boyish mind, but the source from which I had received it, as I said at the beginning of this introductory note, had entirely slipped from my memory.]

SWEET Leddy Maude looked owre the castle wa'
   When daylicht was fauldin' its e'e,
A' doon an' oot owre the hale border road
   Wi' a sorrowfu' face look'd she;
For she'd plichted her troth to young Fernlea—
   A gallant guid, baith brave an' braw,
But her faither's sworn she maun wed ere morn
   Wild Randal, Lord o' Elvinshaw.

Sune she heard laich doon in the court below,
   Through gloamin's fa', mid win' an' weet,
The clatter o' mail, the jingle o' spurs,
   An' the pawing o' horses' feet;
Then her faither's voice, in lood angry tones,
   As he rattled the tirlin' pin—
"Why comesna my scornfu' young dochter Maude
   To welcome bauld Lord Randal in?"

Then wi' tott'ring steps she crap doon the stair,
   Sick at heart, to mak' her ready;
"Why loiter ye, Maude? Gae busk ye, my bairn,
   This nicht ye'll be Randal's leddy."

I

Wi' a hinging heid she gaed slowly ben,
  Wan was she as the lily floe'r,
" I'd raither ye'd brocht me my burial weeds ! "
  She tauld her maids in buskin' bouir.

When the priest was gane an' the feasting dune,
  When guests lay tossing in their dreams,
Frae the bridal bouir o' the new-wed pair
  Cam' gruesome groans an' piercing screams :
There they foun' Maid Maude : her thin hauu's dreep'd
    bluid,
  Lord Randal's life-bluid stain'd the room,
" See, there lies the carle that I wed," she hissed,
  " Noo ye can bed ye're braw bridegroom."

" Tak' up, tak' up, yer brave gallant sae gay,
  An' sweel him weel baith heid an' feet,
For the linen that busks the bridal bed
  Will mak' a denty winding sheet."
She dash'd through them a' as the wild beast bounds
  She took but twa steps to the stair,
Past the startled grooms, through the castle yetts
  She fled as flees the hunted hare.

* * * * * *

When fishers were drawing their nets neist morn,
  Fernlea in dule an' wae walk'd there,
An' they dragg'd droon'd Maude to her luver's feet
  Wi' sea-weed fanklet in her hair.

He looted low doon, kiss'd her clay-cauld lips,
    Nae licht lay in her bonnie een ;
" I tumbled an' toss'd through the lee-lang nicht,
    But dream'dna ye slept here yestreen.

" Is it thus," he sighed, " that my darling Maude
    Has come to keep her tryste wi' me ?
But nae maid shall e'er lie within my airms,
    For sune, my love, I'll follow thee."
Fernlea was laid in the mools by her side,
    The Laird ne'er lifted heid ava,
An' a' wha took pairt in that wearie weird
    Hae been lang, langsyne wede awa.

Scarce a stane noo staun's o' the castle wa's,
    For Time's teeth ha'e crumbl'd them sair,
The moss has been growing owre a' their graves
    Three hundred years, I trow, an' mair ;
Yet the place is shunn'd by baith auld an' young
    As sune as fa's the gloaming gray,
For Leddy Maude walks in " The Haunted Keep,"
    They will tell ye until this day.

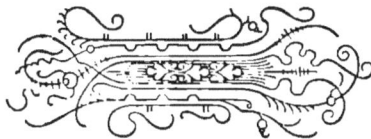

The Doleful Lady and the Boding Bird.

THE steeds of the ocean were tossing their manes,
　　And pawing the roots of the perilous peak,
　　Where a vulture— that ominous bird of doom—
Croaked and whetted the edge of its bended beak ;
While the huge waves swept dashing across the bay,
　　Like onset of battle, with clashing of swords,
A pale lady stept over the oozing sands,
　　With her sad thoughts growing to boding words.

" Oh, bird, croaking so loud from your eyrie's height,
　　Who now peereth so fierce through the twilight gray,
With a hungering look in your demon eyes,
　　Have you feasted your ravenous brood to-day ?
For while darkness is falling o'er all the land,
　　And goes hiding the face of the tumbling sea,
Your harsh screamings sweep past on the whistling blast,
　　Now, what ills you are dreaming of tell to me."

Then the bird ceased whetting its scimitar beak,
　　While a weird, lurid light in its eyes did gleam,
And firm poised on the cliffs with its clasping claws,
　　Seem'd to answer the maid with a croaking scream :
" Of the low gurgling shrieks in a sinking ship
　　That dropt down fathoms deep as it neared the bay,
Of the corpses will roll on the sobbing shore,
　　With my beak in their hearts at the dawn of day."

When she heard these sad words from the boding bird,
　　Oh, more pale grew the lady and sad to see,
For now shatter'd like grass from a baby's hand
　　Lay the dreams whose fulfilling would never be.

" Love and hope now sunk down with that ship," she said,
　" For my lover speeds homeward across the sea,
And with wealth of pure gold from the far-off lands,
　He is coming to make a glad bride of me."

But the croaking bird scream'd, " See your bridegroom
　　comes
　From the waves ; he is tossing about your feet,
Then lean down, lift him up as a gift from me,
　And your bride robes will make him a winding sheet."
But none ever may tell through that night of storm
　How sore grief at her heart-strings then tugg'd and tore,
For her shrieks were all drown'd by the howling winds,
　And the dirge at her death was the tempest's roar.

From ebbing and flowing of tides on the beach,
　And where wreckage toss'd drifting, they found her there
With her lover lock'd fast in her clasping arms,
　And the sea tangle twining among their hair.
Where yon nettles grow rank in the churchyard mould,
　And the low bending willows above them weep,
In one peaceful grave the fond lovers rest,
　Till the last trump shall wake them they soundly sleep.

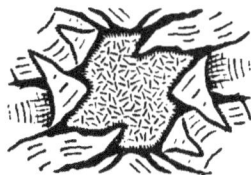

The Weary Wuds o' Gloom.

THE wearied sun was sinking slow oot —owre the
        "Wuds o' Gloom,"
    An' seem'd within a sea o' bluid to wauchle an' to
        soom ;
The birds sat cooring on the trees, their lilting sangs were
    dune,
    The eerie lichts had whisper'd them a storm was coming
        sune.
They heard it muttering in its dreams, ere it in fury woke,
    To bellow wi' its thousand tongues frae every echoing
        rock ;
An' there, where miles o' heath, an' fern, and craigs sae
    bleak an' bare,
    For ages watch the hoary wuds stretch up their airms in
        prayer,
Close hiding in a hillside lirk, amid the gathering gloom,
    Pale Lady Margaret sat an' grat beneath a bush o' broom.

While thus she sabb'd her life awa', wi' bitter rain o' tears
    The clatter o' a horse's hoofs broke on her listening ears,
An' doon the windings o' the cleuch, a horseman grim she
    saw,
    Speed here an' there, wi' muttered oaths, into the west
        awa.
Wi' wullcat een she watch'd an' saw him passing frae her
    sicht,
    Then moan'd an' mumbled to hersel' amid the fading
        licht ;
"Gang on yer gate, my ance guidman," puir Margaret
    sabbit sair,
    " For in the circling o' yer airms ye'll rock me never mair.

Ye ca'd me wanton in yer cups, afore yer crooded ha',
I flung ye back oor wadding ring, then swiftly sped awa,
I kiss'd oor bairnies in their dreams an' left them sleeping
there,
Noo for your sin, I mak' my bed, wi' foumart an' wi'
hare.

" Yestreen, through a' the weary nicht, amid the rain an'
sleet,
I heard oor bairns cry ' mither,' an' I heard them sab an'
greet;
Oh would that they were wi' me noo, a' gather'd closely
roon,
An' in the dreamless trance o' death, we a' were sleeping
soun'.
We'd maybe wauken up, made pure through suffering an
through pain,
An' a' the love slips bye us noo, be gather'd back again;
But here I'm havering in the dark, the daylicht's nearly
fled,
It's time the weans had aff their claes an' hush-a-ba'd to
bed—
Lay doon yer drums, yer bows an' swords, an' a' yer haps
an' cares,
An' noo afore ye'll cuddle doon I'll hear ye say your
prayers."

"Yes, ' wanton,' was his cruel word," she raved an' moaned
again,
" I would hae drain'd my heart-bluid dry to save my lord
frae pain;

His pure an' spotless wedded wife, that thing o' dread an'
    shame
  At thocht o't still my freezing bluid bursts into fire an'
    flame.
Noo since love's dream has pass'd an' gane, there's naething
    left for me
  But hide the ' wanton ' frae his sicht an' hurkle doon
    an' dee ;
Noo kiss me bairns afore ye sleep, come kiss me ane an a',
  Sweet Bessie, Kate, an' Margaret, an' my brave laddies twa;
Or ye can don yer claes ance mair an' gather roon my feet,
  I'll tell ye tales will mak' ye lauch, an' sangs will gar ye
    greet.

Noo mind ye what I say, my bairns, an' mak' my word yer
    law,
  Act kindly to yer faither, weans, when I am taen awa ;
But whist-noo-whist, what's this I hear—I hear the roll o'
    drums,
  A gran' procession passes an' the King in Glory comes.
He reaches oot His glittering haun an' lifts me to His side,
  An' leads me to His palace there for ever to abide ;
His glory comes atween us noo an' hides ye frae my sicht,
  Sae I maun bid ye a' my bairns a lang an' last 'guid-
    nicht ;'
But dae yer best, my bonnie bairns, an' come ye late or sune,
  I'll wait ye a' owre yonder when life's weary warsel's
    dune."

By this the storm had broken loose, the lichtning fierce did
    play,
  Struck deid within a lanely cleuch the waunerin' horse-
    man lay ;

At morn when searchers cam' to search the weary " Wuds
    o' Gloom,"
    They found " My Leddy " stark an' stiff beneath a bush
        o' broom.
An' since that sad an' dreary nicht o' dule, an' flude, an'
    flame,
    Their keep has crumbled into dust, their memory's but a
        name.
But while adoon the stream o' Time the centuries swiftly
    run,
    The tale I've told has been re-told from white-haired sire
        to son ;
And still the hinds on nichts o' storm talk o' her gruesome
    doom,
    And whisper—" Noo ' The Leddy ' walks the weary
        ' Wuds o' Gloom.' "

Forsaken.

OH, wheesht! for yer greeting I canna thole,
　　An' gi' me ae moment's peace,
　For my heid is het as a bleezing coal,
An' I can get nae release.
But the waters o' death a' roon me flow
　That sune will slocken this flame
That scorches me noo, whaur I'm lying low,
　Wi' a stain upon my name.

Sae firmly his love-tales I did believe,
　Lown-sweet, like the cushat's croon ;
But fond women will trust an' men deceive
　While this auld gray warl' spins roon.
For like words frae God seem'd his wiling words,
　I lo'ed him sae fondly well ;
But oh! noo they burn me like flaming swords
　Frae the nethermost pit o' Hell.

I'll no curse yer faither, my yaum'rin' bairn,
　Though my heart be sad an' sair—
Though mine was o' wax an' his was o' airn ;
　An' I'll never see him mair.
He'll fauld me nae mair in his airms again ;
　Yet God grant he ne'er may dree
Sic like wearie weird as this racking pain,
　That's gnawing the life frae me.

But I'll slip awa' an' dig a deep grave
　In the Langton wuds sae green ;
Or we'll hide for aye in some lanesome cave
　Where we'll never mair be seen.

But I'm raving noo, for in deidly grips
  I lie like a lump o' lead,
An' couldna lift ye, my bairn, to my lips,
  Though the grave-claes smoor'd yer head.

But when in the mools we drap aff life's load,
  We yer faither's name will lay
At the fit o' His throne, in the ear o' God,
  An' he'll guide the wand'rer's way.
An' we yet may meet in His land sae bricht,
  Wi' oor garments cleans'd frae sin,
Where there's nae mair nicht an' a' wrangs made richt,
  An' the angels' sangs begin.

A' life's warsle an' farsle will sune be past,
  For I'm wearing fast awa';
An' I feel death's mantle aboot me cast,
  Ice-cauld, like a wreath o' snaw.
My soul keeps shaking life's bars to be free,
  Since fate broke love's witching spell :
A' the bonnie braid yirth grew bare for me,
  An' toom as an empty shell.

Oh, joy ! noo my feet touch the gowden stair,
  The wearyfu' pain has ceased ;
Lay me doon, laigh doon, in oor kirkyard lair,
  Wi' my baby on my breist.
An' when I am lying there cauld an' deid,
  Oh ! mither, noo, dinna greet ;
Plant sweet thyme an' violets at my heid,
  An' the daisies at my feet.

An' sometime, maybe no sae lang frae this,
 In the swiftly-speeding years,
He I lo'ed sae weel may come back to kiss
 An' water my grave wi' tears ;
And when there, wi' his heid boo'd doon ye see
 Him greet owre my fun'ral cairn,
Lay yer loof in his, an' oh' then forgi'e
 The faither o' my sweet bairn.

Thus pardoning him wi' her latest breath,
 She slipt frae oor side awa' ;
Sic a bonnie flower booing doon to death,
 Oh, my auld e'en never saw.

The Gruesome Burd.

A FRIAR GRAY on his hameward way
    Frae some scene o' grief an' murning,
    Was met by a Raven gruesome an' grim
  Frae some feast o' bluid returning.
Said the Friar : " Yer lang beak's dreeping wi' gore
    Foul burd, wi' the demon's een,
An' a yer breast feathers are draiggelt owre ;
    Noo at what deils wark hae ye been ?"

" Ho ! Ho ! Ho ! Ho ! " croaked the Raven sae grim,
    As it perched on 'The Suicides' Tree,'
" Oh they needed ye sair whaur I gaed yestreen,
    An' a gruesome sicht did see ;
Yestreen while doon by a clear deep pool,
    To my shadow was becking low ;
I spied a man in a newk o' the wud
    Stalk gloomily to an' fro.

An' ere lang a brave youth past the plantin's edge
    Cam' lilting this stave o' a sang :
Oh my true luve looks oot frae her bouir window,
    An' thinks that I'm tarrying lang.
But he sang nae mair for the lurking man
    Oot ahint him sprang pell-mell
Wi' ae gash in his throat an' three in his hert,
    He murder'd him whaur he fell.

Then hid him frae sicht an' left nae trace
    That ever sic deed had been,
But I scrapit the leaves aff the murder'd man,
    An' howkit oot baith his een.

Gang up then, priest, to the maid who waits,
    Wi' this news frae the corbie-craw,
'On this yirth again she'll see nae mair
    The young Laird o' Hostlerha'.

An' bid her tak' tent o' her cousin Hugh,
    Fause coward sae dour an' grim ;
For he it was spilt her true luve's bluid,
    An' sae foully murder'd him."

But better his fate lying stark i' the wud,
    Than to dree oot yon murd'rer's life ;
For the curse will follow him nicht an' day,
    Till his ain throat sheathes his knife.
An' the lureing sirens o' Lust an' Greed
    Will aroon him weave their spell,
Till he wake frae their witching dreams o' delicht,
    In the seething fires o' Hell.

Oh woe for the dame wha in widow's weeds,
    Murns her deid luve nicht an' day !
An' noo for the peace o' her troubled soul,
    Let all good Christian's pray.

Supping Kale wi' the Deil.

H, my auld Granny's sayings wi' wisdom were rife,
   When a wee lad I learn'd them an' used them
      through life ;
An' there's ane o' her proverbs I mind unco weel,
Was " Ane needs a lang spune that wad sup wi' the Deil."
But though some fowk will argue there's nae Deil ava,
An' we strive whiles to " let that flee stick to the wa' ; "
Yet the puir hunted rough, or rich, rollicking chiel',
Tak's a thocht noo an' then hoo he'll dodge frae the Deil ;
For in spite o' their brag to their cost they ken weel,
Faith—" Ane needs a lang spune that wad sup wi' the
   Deil."

      O, my auld Granny spak' words o' wisdom atweel,
      Mind, " Ane needs a lang spune that wad sup wi'
         the Deil."

Tam M'Scatter was ane o' a froliesome crew,
Wi' a fat reaming purse an' a big aumrie fou :
Heck an' manger wi' him, fill up fou an' fetch mair,
He'd nae ruggings wi' hunger, nae battles wi' care,
But I'm vex'd sair to say sune the maut drooned the meal,
An' juist left him a puir drucken, dotterin' chiel',
While his fine simmer frien's an' flash leddies sae braw
Ane by ane frae his side like lash'd hounds slunk awa'.
A' his fule fauts were talk' o', his ance honoured name
To the hale toon a hissing an' byeword became ;
An' the gom'ral, owre late, to his sair cost ken'd weel,
That " Ane needs a lang spune that wad sup wi' the Deil."

    Oh, my auld Granny spak', &c.

But its waesome to speak o' an' lost time to tell
A' the woes an' mishaps to ae puir cuif befell ;
I could name them by dizzens, ye ken them as weel,
Wha hae tried but got burnt supping kale wi' the Deil.
Sae noo, comrades, I warn ye, tak' tent an' beware,
Lest or ever ye ken ye coup into some snare,
An' then fin' yersel's tied like a stirk in a creel,
An' swift borne off by imps to sup kale wi' the Deil,
But be faithfu' an' manly an' honest an' true,
An' the auld Deil's as guid as a deid Deil to you.

    Yet my auld Granny spak', &c,

A Sumpb an' a Fule.

WHEN I'd juist donn'd my first pair o' breeks
  Ae day I heard faither an' mither,
    When they thocht there was naebody near,
  Hae a queer-like crack wi' each ither.
"Oor Tam's juist a gomeral, guidwife,
  An' I'm fear'd maist to sen' him to schule ;
For the bairns will fin' oot afore lang
  That he's baith a saft sumph an' a fule."

Chorus.

  I keep mind what my auld faither said—
    "He's a saft easie-oozie—he'll be
  Whaure'er he may gang, be't short road or lang,
    Juist a sumph an' a fule till he dee."

When at schule I fell deeply in love
  Wi' the brawest big lassie was there,
An' I bocht her a braw jumpin' jack,
  An' some candy I brocht frae the fair ;
But I nearly drapt doon through the grun',
  The weans were a' lauchin' thegither,
When she said, "Tak' them back, ye big fule,
  Gang hame for a sook to yer mither."

  Chorus—I had a mind what, &c.

I aye was a deil for the lassies,
  Though mony a love-ploy miscarried,
I at last made it up wi' "Oor Jean,"
  A braw, sonsy lass, an' got married ;

K

But when safe in a hoose o' oor ain,
    I said, " Wife, yer a brave ane an' cule,
That could wed, bed, an' kipple for life
    Wi' a saft, simple sumph an' a fule."

      Chorus—I had a mind what, &c.

An' through life, baith at hame or ootbye,
    I've redd mony a wearifu' spule,
For if e'er amang company I gang,
    Fowk aye try to get fun frae the fule.
Faith, I've ne'er cut my wisdom-teeth yet,
    For I'm aye juist the same simple fule
They ance tried to ding lair in lang syne
    Wi' the dominie's mell at the schule.

      Chorus—It was true what, &c.

Ere I bid ye guid nicht, an' sit doon,
    Here's a toast to "The Fules Far an' Near,"
An' be sure they'll never dee oot,
    For I see juist a crood o' them here.
Weel noo, chaps, here's " Guid Frien'ship to a',"
    Sae drink oot an' we'll fill up the cog,
Though I may be "a sumph an' a fule,"
    Yet I'm neither a thief nor a rogue.

      Chorus—Though 'twas true what, &c.

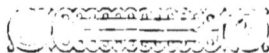

The Basket of Greens.

This rhyme was run off extempore on seeing a very fine statuette
of stucco, representing an old monk seemingly bowed down with the
weight of a heavy basket of vegetables, but when the back of
the wicker basket was slipped back a beatiful female figure was discovered safely concea'ed at bottom of the same.

TO do penance for sin,
    Once a monk took the road,
And he swelter'd and puff'd
    With the weight of his load,
Which, in language most plain,
    Hinted " bacon and beans ;"
For the strange load he bore,
    Was a basket of greens.

So wherever he went
    He found both bed and board,
For the sake of the saints
    And the love of the Lord.
But Priest Joseph had pack'd
    (He found both ways and means)
Food for body and soul
    In his basket of greens.

And here you see plain
    What was smuggled incog,
In his close wicker cage
    By this lecherous rogue,
Who, doom'd for aye, sprawls
    Through Hell's sulphurous scenes,
For the pranks he once played
    With this basket of greens.

M'Pherson's Kye.

NCE on a time, but in my rhyme
    I'll no fix day or date, man,
Nor vouch it true, but jist to you
    A simple tale relate, man ;
For like maist cracks on far-off facts
    In veritable history.
Heigh in the cluds or den'd in wuds,
    The ends are fring'd wi' mystery.

But 'twas a time when rieving crime
    Let lowse the fludes o' passion,
When fowk speil'd braes gie scant o' claes,
    Ere breeks had come in fashion,
Twa gruesome chaps wi' towsie taps,
    Ae gloaming did forgather ;
An' glowering roon, bare houghs boo'd doon
    Amang the blooming heather.

" Weel, did ye hear ? " ae rogue did speir,
    " O' yon took place owreby, man,
Hoo Pate the chief an' Rab the thief
    Hae stown M'Pherson's kye, man ?
An' fine I ken whaur in the glen
    The hale herd rowtes an' rairs, man ;
If you'll agree we'll let them see
    They're as much oors as theirs, man."

Sae said, sae dune, a blinkin' mune
    Juist ser'd their purpose rarely ;
But as through bogs crap hame the rogues
    They lair'd and floundered fairly ;

An' tugg'd and tore, and yell'd and swore—
   Sic sight was never seen, man—
Till ewes an' stots sped aff like shots,
   An' vanish'd frae their een, man.

Though they for days had limp'd the braes,
   Forfoughten-like an' lame, man ;
Noo fleet as harts an' lame, man ;
   They took the road for hame, man.
Neist morn Mac. raise an' donn'd his claes,
   His fruitless quest to try, man ;
When in an' oot a' roon aboot,
   There lay his sheep an' kye, man.

"Preserve us a', what's here ava ?
   Can this be what it seems, man ?
Come oot, ma freens, jag me wi' preens,
   I'm in the land o' dreams, man !
Yet though I say I'm prood this day,
   To get my kye an' sheep, man ;
Some rogues I fear hae foun' stown gear
   Was raither hard to keep man."

Laird Ralston's Wooing.

LAIRD JOHN o' the Ralston cam' up to the gate,
    An' he said he cam' neither to steal nor beg;
        But fidged an' gaed on at a pitifu' rate—
Like a clockin' hen wi' a happity leg.
Quo' I: "Laird, my faither's awa' to the toon,
    An' mither's step't into Miss Broon's owre-bye."
"I saw them gang oot, sae I ventured doon,"
    Said the auld pawkie carle, sae sleekit an' sly.

"Noo, Peggy, my lassie, I've lo'ed ye for lang—
    We've ken'd ane anither for mony a year;
An' I'm juist on the edge o' my harvest thrang,
    Sae my errand the nicht, noo, ye needna' speir,
Wha trusts fremmit fowk ha'e nae sorrows to seek,
    Ye'd hardly believe't, though on oath ye were tell'd,
Though they muckit the byre but twice in the week,
    Yon hizzies wad think wi' hard work they were fell'd.

I ne'er was sae fix'd since the hour I was born:
    Od! my heid's in a creel, an' I'm nearly deid,
Juist say 'Aye,' an' I'll haun' in the cries the morn,
    For some ane maun keep them gey ticht by the heid.
I'm sair needin' a wife doon at Ralston Ha';
    An' I've rowth o' guid siller, an' sheep an' kye;
Sae juist step yer ways yont an' ye'll get them a',
    An' owre an' aboon get mysel' forbye."

" Laird John was a sensible sort o' a chiel,
    An' no sic an ill lookin' mannie ava' ;
An' I ken't he had lo'ed me baith lang and weel,
    Sae I hadna' the heart juist to say him 'Na.'
An' he look'd sae forfoughten an' sair forlorn,
    I'm e'en gaun to risk it whate'er may betide,
Three times we've been cried, an' the wadding's the morn
    Step ben an' ye'll get a bit dram frae the bride."

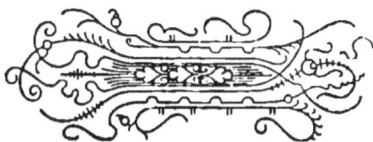

Tiglath=Pileser.

(See 2nd Kings, 15th Chapter, 29th Verse.)

Strange that a king who helped to make or mould as much of
the young world's history should be so utterly forgotten in this. If
we are to believe the records of his contemporaries, who have
written his wonderful deeds and achievements in hieroglyphics on
the rocks of Egypt, we must believe more wonderful things were
done by him than almost any of these old conquering heroes we are
more familiar with. Within the last century so many of these
inscriptions have been translated for our benefit that the difficulty
now remains with us to compress all these wonderful deeds into the
lifetime of one man. In confirmation of this, I would merely refer
my readers to the pages of Layard, Smith, Bonomi, or any other of
these learned men who have made this branch of study their life
work. Now, in spite of all this evidence, I was gravely informed,
by one moving in most respectable circumstances, the other day that
such a king never existed, and yet this did not surprise me, knowing
the "trifles light as air" with which our young, and I am grieved
to say older, men are puffed up. I thoroughly believe were anyone
to propound the question, "Who was Tiglath-Pileser?" in a
mixed company of fifty people, not five of the number could answer
correctly. Knowing this, I began the following rhyme in a bantering
spirit, but gradually, as the rhymes rushed on me, there came a
sense of the mutability of all earthly things, and how swiftly a few
years hide from the memory of men even the very names of many
who seemed destined to hold an abiding place till the end of time.
Though forgotten of men let us live in the faith that God will write
our names in His Book of Life.—J. H.

THEY'D sic queer names or phrase
    In thae auld Bible days—
Tak', for instance, Rabshakeh, or Nebuchadnezzar,
    Artaxerxes, an' mair,
    But there's few can compare

Wi' that King wi' the strange name of Tiglath-Pileser,
    Tiglath-Pileser, Tiglath-Pileser,
Wi' that lang-nebbit name o' King Tiglath-Pileser.

    An' to coort wi' at mirk,
    Or to ask to the kirk
For a wife (wi' sic name) ane wha didna say " Nay,
    sir ; "
    But sae weel did he plead
    She soon cuddled her heid
On the braid, brawny briest o' young Tiglath-Pileser ;
    Tiglath-Pileser, Tiglath-Pileser,
She got wedded an' bedded to Tiglath-Pileser.

    Was she dark ?   Was she fair ?
    An' yet what need we care ?
It's owre late in the day noo to blame her or praise
    her ;
    Or to tell hoo she look'd,
    When her friend's their mou's crook'd
While striving to say—" Mrs Tiglath-Pileser ;"
    Tiglath-Pileser, Tiglath-Pileser,
She had cronies nae doot, " Mrs Tiglath-Pileser."

    But this fierce fechting chiel,
    At his chariot wheel,
Brocht Israel captive ; their wealth he did lay, sir
    In the pomp o' his pride,
    At the feet o' his bride,
As a honeymoon gift frae King Tiglath-Pileser ;
    Tiglath-Pileser, Tiglath-Pileser,
For a sad rieving loon was this Tiglath-Pileser.

Then puir Judah's bairns sat
By the waters an' grat,
For afore a' the nations he tried to debase her;
When to bondage they came
And in sackcloth an' shame
Were made vassals and serfs to King Tiglath-Pileser;
Tiglath-Pileser, Tiglath-Pileser,
Oh, the pitifu' times o' King Tiglath-Pileser!

But they're lang deid an' gane
Doon deith's dreich road their lane,
To some places ye'll no fin' in "Murray" or "Frazer,"
For owre Charon's dark burn
Nae late swift trains return,
Sae I canna sae mair aboot Tiglath-Pileser;
Tiglath-Pileser, Tiglath-Pileser,
But they made a gran' mummy o' Tiglath-Pileser.

Doon oor new world's track
Could his leddy look back,
We could show her some new things I'm sure wad
    amaze her;
But the het desert's san'
Has for ages been blawn
In heaps owre baith her an' King Tiglath-Pileser;
Tiglath-Pileser, Tiglath-Pileser,
Owre that ance famous King they ca'd Tiglath-Pileser.

Noo his name's but a name,
In oor strivings for fame,
Dae the warld some guid an' frae some dub up-raise her
For life's short at the best,
Sune the grave-clods will rest,

As firm owre oor heids as owre Tiglath-Pileser ;
    Tiglath-Pileser, Tiglath-Pileser,
We are coming to meet you King Tiglath-Pileser.

    Then let's watch an' tak' heed
    O' ilk word an' ilk deed,
For maist surely an' swift comes death's reckoning day,
    sir,
    When riches or fame
    Drap like moths frae a flame,
An' the slave in the grave equals Tiglath-Pileser ;
    Tiglath-Pileser, Tiglath-Pileser,
Noo time's dust an' its mist hide King Tiglath-Pileser.

The Kangaroo.

NONSENSE RHYMES.

LEDDY PEGGY got up ae dark morning at three,
  When the weazles were playing a tune,
An' she made a fish supper o' twa pigs' feet,
  An' wi' sparables tackit them doon.
While her ninety years' lover, Sir Barnaby Bobbs,
  On his ring-tail'd cuddy an' four,
Stood up on his heid an' turned ten cairt wheels
  To John Anderson's wife at the door.

Chorus—

" Noo let's dance an' sing in a four-square ring,"
  A' the cocks frae the steeples crew ;
"Then on snails an' whales an crocodiles' tails
  We will feast," said the Kangaroo.

But the green girning monkey wee Totum-in-Breeks
  Saw the elephant dibbeling kale,
Sae he preen'd black puddings as strong as goats
  To the potted-heid crocodiles' tail.
Then the hale crood danced a Mexican waltz,
  While the cocks their chanters blew ;
But what means this blether o' rhyme ?
  Speir that at the Kangaroo.

Chorus—

" Noo let's dance an' sing in a four-square ring," &c.

Potiphar's Wife.

AE day I had opened the brods o' *The Beuik*
　　To wale for some words that wad guide me through
　　　　life,
When the first kittle chapter I happened to read,
　Was the story o' Joseph an' Potiphar's Wife.
It's a story we've a' mumbled owre at the schule,
　An' its wasted time, ye say, sic auld tales to rehearse,
But wi' your permission i'll tell't owre again,
　In a hap-an-step stave a' lame rambling verse.

Noo ye a' ken hoo Joseph was sold for a slave,
　An' his maister, the Captain, sune loed him sae wee.,
That he gied him full charge baith inside an' outbye,
　But his mistress was juist a vile limb o' the deil.

　　　　She saw Potiphar auld
　　　　Had grown doited an' cauld,
　　　　An' young Joseph was yauld
　　　　Wi' a guid grip o' life ;
　　　　But she ogled in vain
　　　　His love gifts to obtain,
　　　　For an oot-an'-oot limmer
　　　　Was Potiphar's wife.

When he fled frae her grups she to Potiphar said—
　" See what Joseph your flunkey has dune unto me :
　　　　He has toozled me sair,
　　　　An' he micht hae dune mair,
　　　　Sae I vow an' declare,
That this day he maun dee."

Sae this venomous jaud
Raved till Joseph she had
In a dungeon laid fast, whaur he languish'd for
    lang;
But his chains prov'd a stair
To King Pharaoh's side, where
He cocked his bannet the nobles amang.

But why seek in Egypt for jauds when we ken,
    It's a pitifu' fact that sic limmers are rife?
For in less than twa miles frae oor ain burgh cross,
    I could wale oot a dizzen like Potiphar's wife.
Unstable an' fause as the quicksands o' Dryfe,
    Wha sae vex an' perplex their puir husbands through
        life,
They could whiles wish them banish'd to Freuchie-in-Fife.

But, like Joseph's, oor ills may turn roon for oor guid,
Though o' weed an' o' tares we've a plentyfu' crap;
If we keep a firm grup o' the haun' guides us on,
Though the deil tries us sair weel aye soom to the tap.

Leddy Evergreen.

EDDY EVERGREEN leeves in a street in this toon
In its cosiest spot she has planted her doon,
But oh ! sic a prood taid I'm sure never was seen,
As this upstart frae naething—this Dame Evergreen.

Now the cabin, ould Dorby, her faither, had bocht,
Stood where some improvements were gaun to be
wrocht,
As the wiseacres said for the guid o' the toon,
Sae they paid him some gowd an' the biggin dang doon.

This laid oot to guid int'rest brocht twa croons a week,
Sae wi' this splendid pension, an' plenty o' cheek,
Wi' some new falderals an' silk china-blue dress,
Oor Miss Judy set up for a Leddy—nae less.

An' when ould Dorby died the swate darling Bo-Peep,
Losh, she louted sae low that she lifted a sweep,
But puir Pat sune fan' oot 'stead o' ane he'd got twa,
For he'd wed baith a wife an' a mither-in-law.

Noo puir Paddy the sweep, ance sae tatter'd an' torn,
Wad fain claim to be kin' to the Marquis o' Lorne,
Or that famous auld sodger o' valour an' micht,
That ance led oor braw Kilties up Alma's red heicht.
But the Flaherty's, Tooles, or rint paying o' grumph,
Are but britheren a' to puir Paddy the sumph.

We see mony a man as we daunder through life,
  Mak' a fule o' himsel' for his doll o' a wife,
A fine swatch o' thae cuifs that sweer, bounce, cringe or
      creep,
  As their better hauf bids is puir Paddy the sweep.

For this saft, simple chiel, quate, an' mim as a mouse,
  Snooves an' snools oot an' in through his pairt o' the
      hoose,
For ony man's corner ye ken maun be but sma'
  That is ruled by a wife an' a mither-in law.

Now this Brummagem-jewel'd sweep's dawty an' pet
  Is that scunnersume thing ca'd "a marrit coquette,"
An' the fowk when she passes say, smirking like mad,
  "There's the Evergreen on her daily peraud."
Though she tries wi' her grandeur to dazzle their een,
  There's but few that tak' up wi' this Dame Evergreen.

Watch her cleckin' o' weans marshall'd oot in a raw,
  The're a' deck'd oot in duds sae ootrageously braw,
Wi' their prood mincing steps, it's a sicht to be seen,
  For they a' ape their mither, the Dame Evergreen.

If ye're oot for a daunder jist step doon the street
  Whaur she leeves ; at her window ye'll see sic a treat
A wheen babby-clouts buskit wi' ribbons an' tape,
  Like a muckle craw bogle stuck up on a graip,
To fricht his fowk awa an' sic wauf rift-raff core
  O' puir beggars far back frae her majesty's door.

Hoots ! I'm wrang saying this, for ae month in the year,
    His wee auld wizzen'd mither gets leave to draw near,
The red star-spangled chaummers to dust an' keep clean,
    While wi' flocks "doon the wanter" trips Dame Ever-
        green.
O'd it saves a month's wages—sma pairins mak' bien
    An' a wee cek's a help to this Dame Evergreen.

But this simmer while doon at her sea-side retreat,
    To a leddy I ken she sent oot an inveet
To ca' in, but gat leeve in her mixture o' blooms
    Jist to chew her ain cud an' to twiddle her thooms.
For the highly respectables widna be seen
    Hacin giff-gaff wi' upstarts like Dame Evergreen.

Guid help ony man's bairn that comes under their claw,
    For the auld hen an' young hen sae cackle an' craw
They sune deave ony quate, decent lassie awa,
    Wi' their tongues foul click-clack that like mill-happer
        rins,
For a judgment to punish her manifold sins,
    She's in limbo sax weeks wi' this supple-tongued queen,
Syne she's hame like a shot frae this Dame Evergreen.

But I trow on sic puir Lilliputians sae sma',
    It's waisterie o' time to spoil paper ava,
Did I no think she stood as a swatch o' that class,
    Think genteelity lies in a braw silken dress,
An' their puir simple servant is jist a kick-ba,
    An' are scarce o' the same God's creation ava,

I hae aye taen the puirs pairt, an' wull, in despite
   The gur-wurring o' upstarts, their bark or their bite,
An' while health guides my pen, or licht lauchs in my een,
   Wrang an' folly I'll tramp on where e'er they are seen,
Be't in King, Duke, or Duchess, or Dame Evergreen.

Gone Home.

THOUGH loath to leave pale weeping friends,
　　The voice of God had said " Arise,
　See where above your drooping head
　The banner of Salvation flies.
Lift up those far-off dreaming eyes,
　　Ye go not in the dark alone ;
My angels compass thee about,
　　And they will safely guide you on."

" Lord, Thou hast call'd, I come," she said,
　　Then meekly bow'd her weary head
Upon the bosom of The Christ,
　　And neighbours whisper'd " She is dead."
But from that chrysalis of death,
　　The prison'd soul had found its wings ;
And richer grown with robes of faith,
　　Than earth with all its crowns and kings.

And as they pass'd the gates of beryl,
 The heav'nly harpers clear and strong
With joy for one more soul redeem'd,
 Broke forth in ecstasies of song.
They put the new song in her mouth,
 Now, free from care, and pain, and tears:
Her anthem round the great white throne
 Flows through the everlasting years.

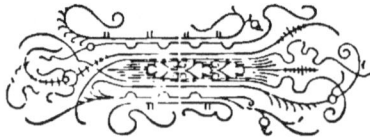

The Rev. Robert Kerr.

Lines to the memory of the Rev. Robert Kerr, who died at
Wakefield, Kansas, on Sunday, 29th June, 1890. A true Christian
minister and genial poet, and whom for many years John Hyslop
was proud to call his counsellor and friend.

A LINK that caught the present time,
    And chain'd it to the years gone by,
    And music struck from Memory's chime
Low as Goliath now doth lie.
Dear friend—dead friend, now laid so low,
    By strangers in a distant land,
It seems but yesterday we stood
    Here, face to face, hand clasp'd in hand.

And talk'd of all the pleasant past,
    And of the fruitful years to come ;
And now there lies your broken harp,
    The music of its song grown dumb,
And you have reach'd " Our Father's " House,
    And through His ever open door,
To hold communion with the saints,
    Goes on a little way before.

Oh ! pitying God, Who notes alike
    The giant's death, the sparrow's fall,
Be present with the mourning ones
    Who from their place of weeping call :
Oh ! dry their tears, and bid them see
    His struggle past, the victory won—
He sings in Glory the New Song
    He had on earth so well begun.

No more his " Leaves frae yont the sea "
   Will cheer us with their kindly words,
Nor glittering sweep of polish'd speech
   Will dazzle like a flash of swords.
But though we miss and mourn him sore,
   And sob with sympathy of pain,
We know his hopes are all fulfill'd—
   Our loss was but his greater gain.

Weak nature, stunn'd beneath the blow,
   May mutter in the dark and say :
" He was so dear while with us here,
   And Heaven seems so far away."
Up and look up, the dark grows light,
   And from the land where he has gone
We see far up the Shining Path,
   His hand to Glory beckoning on.

Sad Bereavements.

DEAR FRIEND, indeed, in need, for thirty years,
  Where you in sackcloth shed your hidden tears
    I dare be bold to say your grief is mine,
And claim the right to mix my tears with thine.
Scoffers may say my muse so dull has grown
It chants but dirges o'er some funeral stone,
But 'tis not so : I bring no words of gloom,
But songs of cheer, and point beyond the tomb,
For past the glamour of Life's grinding wheels—
My soul but utters what it deepest feels.

My hand clasps yours, now, while you nurse your grief,
Where Death stole sudden, like a midnight thief,
In one short week, both Wife and Daughter too;
Oh, tale most pitiful, yet sadly true.
God needed them and called each to her place ;
But though on earth we meet each smiling face,
Till the Day dawn, and shadows flee away
We'll keep their memories in our hearts for aye.

I do not bid you now your tears refrain—
Strength grows from weakness, sunshine follows rain ;
Though dark and cheerless seems life's coming road,
Lay but your burdens at the feet of God.
Dark will grow bright, and from the shining shore
His cords will bind you to those gone before,
And you will soon unclasp your wringing hands
And see again where Work or Duty stands ;
Only look up, hold firm the larger hope
And though you now 'mong clouds and shadows grope,
Time, the consoler, will most sure reveal ;
God's hand ne'er smote yet where it could not heal.

On Seeing the Military Funeral of Sergeant=Major J. Flynn.

DROWNED 24TH OCTOBER, 1891.

NOW, together stepping slowly,
  Into marching orders fall,
There our comrade now lies lowly,
  And we mourn him one and all.
Not in front nor brunt of battle
  Did his honour'd labours cease ;
But the Great Commander call'd him
  In the piping times of peace.

No one knows when death may find them ;
  He from pleasure pass'd from sight,
Swiftly through the land of shadows,
  Let us hope to realms of light.
"Dust to dust" now chant the requiem,
  Loose the chords and lay him in,
We can ne'er find better comrade
  Than we lose in Sergeant Flynn.

Let us not forget the mourners,
  Who so dazed with grief sit dumb,
List'ning to the " Dead March " music,
  And the low tap of the drum.
Soon or late our fates will meet us,
  Be't in peace or battle's roar,
May we be prepared to meet them,
  Like our comrade gone before.
Bury him with soldier's honours,
  O'er him shoot your farewell rounds,
Now " *Requiescat in pace* "
  Till the Grand Reveille sounds.

Lines to the Memory of Eliza Cook.

DIED 24TH SEPT., 1889, AGED 71 YEARS.

[John Hyslop when he penned these verses, accompanied them with the following words :—" At the end of last month there passed quietly to her rest one of England's sweet singers. Her muse had so long been silent we had almost forgotten she lived. Louder and stronger-voiced poets have come to the front during her silence, till her sweet songs have almost faded from the memories of many who in earlier years either sung or listened to the melting music of " The Old Arm Chair," " The Sailor's Grave," " I'm Afloat," " Mary of Castlecarry," and scores of others that have passed into the literature of our country ; and many who sing them now could not tell you their author's name. Pity this should be so ; but when my heart ceases to respond to the brave sweet words of hope and cheer she has left behind in her works, it will have ceased to beat."]

DEAD ! and but yesterday, the singer sweet
    Whose songs of cheer made witchery through
        the land,
Striving to link Love and Faith's chain complete,
  And tone earth's discords to a music grand.
Peace to her shade—wreaths for remembrance bring ;
  Her gentle soul loved everything.

To the weird pathos of her "Old Arm Chair"
  Our souls responding, own'd the power could thrill
With sad, sweet memories, and we follow'd where
  She led and drew us at her own sweet will,
And saw where shams walk'd in their rounds of wrong ;
  She swoop'd and maim'd them with her sword of song.

Strange fierce conceits now storm the public ear,
  Her quavering lark's song we can scarcely hear ;
But give sweet leisure and a quiet nook,
  Then soul to soul talk with ELIZA COOK.
Her pure-soul'd womanhood and cheering words
  Will charm you like a nest of singing birds.
Song never dies—strew flowers her grave upon ;
  Her song through all Eternity rolls on.

"Rue for Remembrance."

—*Hamlet.*

H silent friend, from my own sick bed I
Drop this small wreath where thou dost lowly lie ;
One brief short week since, while we walk'd
together,
Your laugh made sunshine in the stormy weather ;
But fingers beckon'd, and a voice said, "Come !"
Your heart lies frozen and your voice grew dumb
The mysteries of Life and Death you know
Where you have gone, and we must shortly go.

No merrier heart nor readier willing hand
Ever beat or toil'd in any Christian land :
Bird, beast, or man were neighbours great and small—
Your heart of love had room enough for all.
Where now your place no living man can tell,
But this we know, God doeth all things well :
Will cheer the widow in her sore distress,
And be a Father to the fatherless.
We fondly trust He clasp'd your groping hand,
And led you safe into "The Better Land,"
From whence, with clear, calm eyes, you look and see
This wreath I've woven for the love of thee.

To Lord Rosebery.

ON THE DEATH OF HIS BELOVED COUNTESS.

OH! you whose voice with cheering words,
   Rang clarion marches of the free,
  We clasp your hand and mourn your loss,
   We loved your lady, loving thee.
God's Cross of pain doth truly teach,
  That every loss, and every tear,
And all that lifts us up from self,
  But helps to draw the Heavens more near.

God help your sorely mourning maid
  Who "could not make her mind sit down;"
Who by your side, with bow'd head, watch'd
  Death's angel weave the cypress crown.
The whole land mourns your heavy loss;
  Oh! may this load of grief reveal—
Though God's bared arm be sore to smite,
  Yet it is also strong to heal.

Drowned.

LINES IN MEMORY OF MISS HELEN GIBSON.

MID the whirl of pleasure to-day,
　　We in sackcloth sit nursing our pain,
　　　And sore mourning the loss of a dear one,
We on earth will meet never again.
While our bright crowd of holiday-makers
　　Were watching the sea and the ships,
Oh ! the death angel sudden descended,
　　And our mirth had a fearful eclipse.

For a space our small boat, like a feather,
　　Spun round on the foam of the tide,
Then it swamp'd, and we struggled for life,
　　While it drifted away from our side ;
But our sweet little, dear little Nellie---
　　The darling and the flower of the flock—
From the noise of the trouble around her,
　　To the songs of the angels awoke.

We shall miss her so much from our midst,
　　We shall miss the sweet smile of her face,
But we'll cherish her memory through life,
　　Until we also go to our place ;
And we nurse in our souls the sweet hope,
　　When the arm of the Smiter was bared,
And God lifted her up from our side,
　　That she went as one going prepared.

And we trust when our life cares have ended,
And we drift out and on to our fate,
That her fair form will meet us and greet us
When we enter the Beautiful Gate.

She Has Gone like the Snows.

SHE has gone like the snows that have melted
    Before the hot beams of the sun ;
To their rest fold the hands once so nimble,
    For life's toil and its pleasures are done.
Oh, so swift she was struck from before us,
    When the call " Come up hither " was giv'n,
Like an oak storms have shaken for ages
    By the torch of a thunder-bolt riv'n.

How I pity the motherless babies
    That are crying for her through the night,
And she lying so cold in the churchyard,
    And now hidden away from their sight.
But I doubt not she heareth their sobbings
    Where the light of Eternity gleams,
And I know by the joy of their smiling
    She is talking to them in their dreams.

Then look upward, my dear friend and brother,
    For the hand of the Smiter can heal ;
And what seems now in mystery folded
    Soon the opening vail will reveal—
For how nearly we stand to life's ending
    Oh, no living thing ever can know ;
Let us gird up loins and make ready,
    And be waiting the summons to go.

But while life and its duties still wait us,
    Oh, we dare not fold hands and sit dumb ;
Cares and sins must be fought with and baffled
    On our march to the kingdom to come.

Though now bleeding and bruis'd by misfortunes,
  You go groping in gloom and in pain,
Place your hand in the hand of the Healer,
  And be up, man, and at it again.

Soon the smooth hand of Time, the consoler,
  Will make paths through the wilderness road,
And the peace of a mind that is trustful
  Will so lighten your journey to God.
Till at last when life's labours are ended,
  And the past and the present are one,
All our lost, near the feet of " Our Father "
  Will hear his grand welcome " Well done ! "

Anchored!

Lines to the memory of John Gibson, chief mate of s.s. Baron
Elebank, who died after a short illness at Rangoon, Burmah, and
lies buried in the Protestant Cemetery there.   Aged 28 years.

TO those who, for a dear one lost,
　　Now wring their hands in bitter woe,
I fain would whisper words of cheer,
　　And point where healing waters flow.
I do not (like you) mourn the dead,
　　But for the living tears will fall ;
I know poor " Jack " has gone aloft
　　In answer to the Captain's call.

I know while climbing honour's path
　　He grew to be " The Family Pride ; "
God help you in this darken'd hour—
　　God help his sad, unwedded bride.
Though it seems hard to stay the tears
　　That fain would like a river run,
And kneeling at " Our Father's " feet,
　　To whisper " Lord, Thy will be done,"

God doeth all things well, we know,
　　His power is over all the lands ;
He brought your sailor safely where
　　His eyes were closed by kindly hands.
His corpse lies not in ocean depths,
　　Nor where the rock-bound breakers roar,
But sound he sleeps in old Rangoon,
　　Beside the Irriwaddy's shore.

The bul-bul o'er the stranger's grave
  Will come to sing his evening song ;
The thrush from the pagoda domes
  The low, sweet requiem prolong.
Perchance now while you mourn him here,
  From where he wears the starry crown,
To hear your prayers and whisper " Peace,"
  His spirit may be looking down.

Have faith—look up, sad drooping souls,
  And at Christ's feet your burden lay ;
God will " make straight the crooked paths,"
  And " through the wilderness a way ; "
And lead you safe in His good time
  For aye within His fold to be,
Where you will meet your loved and lost,
  And where " there shall be no more sea."

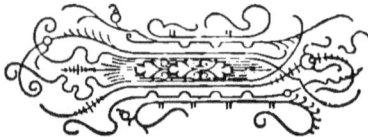

James M'Kie.

Born 1816.—Died 1891.

> " Touch once more a sober measure,
>   And let punch and tears be shed
> For a prince of good old fellows
>   That, alack-a-day ! is dead."
>   —" *Lament for Captain Paton, by J. G. Lockhart.*"

THUS in the century's earlier years
    A poet troll'd his doleful lay
For one, a prince among his peers,
    Like him, we miss and mourn to-day,
Yorrick has gone.   We knew him well ;
    His like again we'll never see ;
But we will to our children tell
    The name and fame of James M'Kie.

We'll miss the click-clack of his staff
    As he went walking up and down,
With cheering word and merry laugh,
    Through all the streets and lanes of town.
As some lone lake in its far deeps
    A star from the high heaven inurns,
So, deep within his soul who sleeps,
    Lay shrined the name of Robert Burns.

His queer, quaint saws, with wisdom fraught,
    He gave not with a canting whine,
But his own thoughts he spake and taught,
    Nor heeded much for yours or mine.

He sought for truth—he hated sham
   And snivelling, sanctimonious phrase ;
Believed no Theosophic cram,
   Nor any mad Mahatma craze.

In all this wide and teeming earth
   There lives no purely perfect thing ;
We halt and stumble from our birth,
   And he was but a *man* I sing.
But see him o'er a social cup,
   Filled " wi' a wee drap barley bree "--
Then the warm heart came bubbling up
   We loved and prized in James M'Kie.

Peace to his shade ! why weep or wail ?
   Draw close the shroud about his brow.
We cannot pierce beyond The Veil,
   He's safe within God's keeping now.
We'll keep his fame from moth or rust,
   And sound his name to future days,
For it can only drop to dust
   With the proud pile he helped to raise.

Where'er the foot of Scotsman turns—
   In every land, on every sea—
They link the name of Robert Burns
   With his disciple James M'Kie.

STORIES

BY

JOHN HYSLOP.

———

THE MORNING STAR.

———

HOO I HAD A CRACK WI'
PHARAOH'S SON.

STORIES.

The Morning Star.

A SCOTCH STORY.

CHAPTER I.

"OD, bless me, whaurawa' this morning, Maggie, sae early," said Tam Dalziel, the joiner's apprentice, to bonnie Maggie Jardine, as they maist ran into ane anither's airms while turning Limping Katie, the sweetie-wife's corner. Tam was hurrying hame for an early breakfast, as his maister had a job wad tak' them into the kintra that day, an' as they couldna coont on their ain time, Tam was stepping alang as if his life depended on his speed o' fit; while Maggie, wi' a step as licht as the roe on the mountains, an' looking as fresh as the morning dew, coming roun' the corner frae the opposite direction, forgather'd wi' ane anither as I hae said. Ere ever Maggie could tak' breath or ken what was the maitter wi' her, Tam's airm had slid roon her waist an' he had imprinted a roozing kiss on her cherry lips, which, as micht hae been seen, Maggie took little pains to resent, for their twa heids gaed thegither maist wi' ae consent, tae the intense amusement o' Limping Katie, wha frae ahint her bourocks o' bannocks, farls o' oat-cake, an' bings o' black-man or gundy, had been taking notes o' the hale affair.

"Noo, that's juist like your impudence, Tam," laugh'd Maggie, wi' her bonnie cheeks blushing up into a colour amaist like the poppies amang the corn; "weel, since ye maun ken, I'm gaun up the length o' the Entirkine Ha' Yetts to meet Leezie M'Kinstray, Annie M'Culloch an' Peggy Watson, an' the four o' us are gaun up to the Big Wud to hae a lang day amang the nits an' slaes, sae if ye're no owre bizzy an' can spare us an' hour or twa in the hin-en' o' the afternune we'll be glad o' yer company, an' ye micht dae waur than gie us a bit lift hame wi' oor basket."

"Depend on me, Maggie my lass, I'll be there; for as sune as we're through wi' this bit job we're gaun to, I'll be amang ye afore ever ye ken ye hae weel begun, sae ta-ta the noo, lass."

Sae, wi' the prospect o' an early meeting afore mony hours gaed by, they baith hurried aff their ain gates.

Tam an' Maggie had been "lad" an' "lass" ever since they had sat side by side on the same bink at the village schule thegither, an' had help'd ane anither on, as best as they could, wi' the lessons they got, sic as they were, frae an' auld snufly, drucken, doited bodie o' a dominie, wha, for maist therty years, aff-an'-on, had steepit his brains in the maut o'

Peggy Pinkerton's yill-hoose till what little learning he ance had slippit awa frae him, an', at the time Tam an' Maggie were attending his classes, he ken'd aboot as little o' what the fowk expected him to teach as the boys an' girls did wha day after day sat on the binks afore him. Mony a time when his heid became owre heavy for him wi' the deil's mixture he had smuggled into his desk in the morning, an' which, under the pretence o' mending the nib of a quill pen, or makin' an entry in his journal, he had been smuggling into himsel' a' forenoon till he hardly ken'd which en' o' him was uppermost, he wad say to the bairns, "Gran' troot in the burn last night; what think ye boys o' gaun oot the day an' trying to guddle a wheen o' them? See an' be in time in the morning." Thae afternune holidays became mair an' mair frequent, an' were rare fun for the bairns, but ae morning when the auld wife, wha for mony a year had swoopit oot the auld rickle o' a room the maister had dignified wi' the name o' " schule," gaed in to do her hauf-hour's cleaning afore the bairns wad gather, she foun' the puir auld dominie wi' his heid doon on the desk stark an' deid, an' an empty bottle lying on the flure at his fit. Oot in the dark nicht, wi' nae helpin' haun' to hand a cup o' water to his lips, he had gane to meet his Maker, an' for mony a lang year noo he has been whaur the Lord wull, leaving naething ahint him but the memory o' his death as a monument o' warning to a' that have had the sense to profit by it. But it wisna aboot the auld dominie I meant to talk when I began this story, but aboot the fortunes o' Tam Dalziel an' bonnie Maggie Jardine. They had baith been born an' brocht up in the village there, their faithers an' mithers being hard-working, puir, honest fowk, wha, wi' mony an up an' doon, had man-aged to bring up big families to man's an' woman's estate, to whom naebody could point the finger o' scorn, or say they were muckle better or waur than their neighbours. Maist o' their brithers an' sisters were married an' in hooses o' their ain, an' Tam an' Maggie were makin' straucht tracks in the same direction, though neither o' them yet had seen eighteen simmers. But it was that afternune at the nitting in the Big Wud brocht things to a crisis wi' them.

Tam had gotten hame frae his kintra job suner than he expected, sae the maister let him aff for the afternune, for he was weel liked, an' a gran' workman, an' before sax months wad be his ain maister. Sae, wi' a fit as licht as a feather, he tript past the Entirkine Ha' Yetts an' intae the wud to meet the bonnie lassie he fully intended, afore the twalmonths were past, to bring hame to a snod, decent doo-cot o' their ain bigging.

Tam an' the lassies made the wuds ring for an hour or twa wi' their daffin' till their baskets were fou' an' reaming owre, an' they were a' on the point o' turning their faces for hame when Maggie, wha, wi' her fit on the trunk o' an auld tree, was trying to reach an extra big cluster abune her heid, owre-balanced hersel', an' the auld tree ruit tumbling owre at the same time left her wi' an ancle sae swollen an' sprained she cudna steer a step wi't though her life had been the forfeit. Tam, lifting her in his strong airms, wi' hers aboot his neck, an' their twa fluttering hearts beating side by side, carried her hame the hale twa miles o' gate as licht in his airms as if she had been a bit three-year-auld babby.

Nicht after nicht he was owre at her mither's to see her, an' afore sax months after, an' afore his ain apprenticeship was finished they had begun to build their nest in real earnest.

Weel, they had a quate an' cozy waddling o't, settled doon real comfortable, an' were unco happy, but somehoo or ither Maggie never seemed to hae a day to dae weel after, an' afore sax months had gane by she was dwining and drooping like a wilted lily.

Mony, an' mony a time Tam wad dauner, wi' her leaning on his airm, up the bonnie burnsides, through the Entirkine Ha' Wuds in the simmer afternunes to hear the music o' the burds an' the bees; feel the scent o' the briers an' the honeysuckles, and to see the hand o' God spreid doon a carpet o' flowers for them to tread on. Ae day they had ventured farther into the wuds, an' nearer the big hoose than they had ever done afore, an, or ever they ken'd they were face to face wi' auld Laird Barton himsel' an' his only son, whose age micht be aboot ten or thereawa'. The boy carried a sling or cat-a-pault in his hand, an' every now an' than wud hurl a pebble frae it at the burds in the branches abune his heid.

Laird Barton was a dour, sour, morose man wha had married late in life, and had teazed the leddy he had made his wife into her grave, sune after the birth o' the boy who now walked by his side. After telling Tam " there's no road this way " he turned on his heel an' left them, but the boy, wanting to hae anither fling at the burds, flung but missed his mark, an' the pebble, glancing off, struck young Mrs Dalziel between the temples, wha fell as if she had been shot. When Maggie fell the auld Laird turned wi' a shade o' remorse on his face, an', telling Tam to carry her up to the Ha', strode on afore to make preparations for their coming ; but Tam, never heeding his words, lifted her up as lichtly an' kindly as if she had been a waunert croodlin'-doo he was warming next his ain heart to keep frae starving. He crapt hame wi' her hinging on his airm in the grey o' the gloaming, an' laid her gently doon on her cozy bed in her ain room ; for it was a room an' kitchen they had, though no gaudily, yet comfortably furnished. While Tam glided saftly oot to seek for assistance o' some kind—Maggie lying there hauf-dazed amang the gathering shadows, thocht hoo mony an' mony a nicht, when Tam thocht she was soon asleep by his side, she had watched the stars as ane by ane they gazed for a little space into the room, then passed on in their grand unceasing round in the fitsteps o' Eternity. Aye, mony a time she had watch'd the darkness flee awa' afore the break-ing o' the dawn, an' heard the burds begin their earliest sang in the tree-taps afore their door, an' the swallows chattering to ane anither frae their nests aboon her window, but "there wull come an end o't a' afore lang," she kept muttering to hersel', as she lay wi' the darkness faulding her roon like a mantle.

Tam wisna lang awa' till he was back wi' an auld widowed auntie o' his ain—as kind an' mitherly a body as ye could hae foun' in a day's walk. A' things, that their ain sweet, kindly natures could possibly think o', were dune for puir Maggie, but lang afore the turn o' the nicht she was talking to the stars an' nameing them ane by ane, as if they were auld frien's, for the shock had been owre muckle for her, an' her ain sair hoor o' trouble had come upon her suner than onybody expected, an' things werena' hauf prepared aboot the hoose for the coming o' "The Wee Stranger." Saft as the fa'ing o' feathers the fitsteps o' the doctor an' the nurse moved aboot the hoose daeing what was maist needfu' in the short time at their command', till, juist as the stars were fadeing oot ane by ane in the lift abune, Maggie was wauken'd back to life wi' the yammmering cry o' her ain wee lassie-wean, as it nestled itsel' to sleep on her bosom. Clasping it close to her sabbing heart she speir'd for Tam, wha, a' through that wearyfu' nicht at the fitstool o' his Maker, had been pouring his woe an' hers into the ear o' a pitying God. Wi' a look o' unutterable love she laid the wee puny mite o' humanity in its faither's airms, an' while Tam, bending doon, kissed her on the broo, as if it had been that o' an angel, she saftly whispered "Tak' it Tam, it's a' I hae to lea ye—ye'll no forget me Tam."

"Forget ye, Maggie—no, till the bluid lappers in my veins, an' my heart lies frozen in the haun' o' death. I'll no forget ye; but we'll meet ye yet up yonder, lass," pointing where the greylicht o' morning was slowly creeping owre the distant hills.

"Look Tam," she whispered again, "a' the stars hae faded oot ane by ane and there's only the bricht an' Morning Star looking doon at us; promise me, whatever name ye ca' oor wee link o' love lying yonder, that her pet name will be 'The Morning Star.'"

An' Tam, whose heart was owre fou' for words, booed his heid in token o' assent, an' Maggie's sperrit on the wings o' faith flutter'd awee, then faded oot frae the watchers' sicht, wi' the fadeing oot o' the Morning Star, an' the licht o' a glorious morning was fludeing the earth when the lang, lang look cam' into Maggie's een, an' a' the licht an' glory had faded oot o' the worl' for puir Tam Dalziel.

CHAPTER II.

EIGHTEEN years hae flown by, laden wi' their burden o' joys an' griefs to the sons an' daughters o' humanity, since last we looked into Tam Dalziel's darken'd hame. Mony a change had ta'en place since then. A railway ran past the village noo, wi' its cozy station-house looking doon at it frae the brae-tap. Limping Katie's wee sweety-shop had blossom'd oot into a big co-operative store wi' twa front windows. A' things had prospered wi' Tam; he was noo the heid joiner in the place, wi' men an' boys working to him, but the hauf o' his hert was lying oot yonder in the grave o' his bonnie Maggie, where, a' through the simmer months, the daisies, pansies, an' forget-me-nots wove themselves into a tapestry o' remembrance, an' the honeysuckle, an' jasmine branches twisted an' twined through the railing that kept it sacred frae the fit o' the profaning stranger. Tam was noo in the very prime o' manhood, and his aim an' en' in life lay in making pleasant paths for the feet o' this ither bonnie Maggie, wha had come to him wi' the fadeing oot o' the licht o' "The Morning Star!"

She was bonnie, some said she was prood, at onyrate she was a high-stepping, distant kind o' a lassie, and was perfectly well aware o' what her looking-glass tell't her.

Auld Laird Barton had been lying side-by-side wi' his wife
for aucht years an mair, an' young Stephen, his son, noo
reigned in his stead, an', wi' his rioting an' junketings, was
making duck's an' drakes o' the sair hain'd siller his faither
had left him, an' a sough ran through the place that he
had been seen, after dark, ae nicht on a lane kintra road,
walking side-by-side wi' bonnie Maggie Dalziel. When her
faither cam' tae ken o't he was neither tae haud nor bin, he
sternly forbade ony further meetings, an' threaten'd to pit
her frae aboot his house if they were persisted in. But in
spite o' a' his warnings, Maggie slipped out ae nicht wi' a
wee bundle beneath her airm, an' didna' come back. An' for
twalmonths and mair her shadow had never darken'd
her faither's door. But on the very nicht o' her eighteenth
birthday she crept hame through a' the bye-roads she kent,
o' sae wretched! sae wan an' wearie! wi' a wee three months'
auld bairn cuddled close to her ain breaking heart. There
was nae need to speir whase bairn it was, for it was a rale
Barton, an' faithered itsel'; an' a braw sturdy callan it was.
When puir Tam saw this waumnert lammie o' his creeping
back to the hame-fauld, in the grey o' the gloaming, his
heart, that he thought had become hardened against her,
melted wi' a great gush o' pity, an' the fludegate o' tears
was opened like the rock in the wilderness afore the wand
o' Moses. Here was a new soul to train, an' a sair wrang
to richt. Hauf through that nicht she sat on the wee
creepie stule at her faither's fit, an' tell't hoo, on that nicht
when she slipped awa frae hame, Stephen an' her were
married in secret, legally married afore witnesses, an' hoo,
for mair than sax months, she had carried her marriage lines
safe in her bosom, but ae morning, when she wauken'd in
strange lodgings, in the midst o' a big toon, they were missing, an' sae was Laird Barton, an' frae that hour forrit she

had never looked upon his face again.

After her wee bairn, Tammie, had been born, in the midst o' strangers, she heard he had married some fine English leddy, an' that they had gane to spend their honeymoon abroad. Sae naething was left for her but to turn her face for hame, like the Prodigal in the parable.

Weel, the gran'-bairn grew up a braw strapping chiel, an' the gran'faither learn'd him his ain trade, an' a' things gaed richt wi' him till he was aboot nineteen year auld. His apprenticeship was oot, an' he was a braw help an' comfort to them baith, till a' at ance, like the bursting o' a thunderbolt, cam the news frae India o' the terrible massacre at Cawnpore.

The thrill o' horror that ran through the land roozed the leonine nature in the hert o' young Tam Dalziel, an' he cudna fauld his hauns at hame while helpless women an' bairns were being foully murder'd oot yonder. Sae, in spite o' a' persuasions to the contrary, he steppit into the neighbouring toon, an', afore the week was oot, he was " listed, tested, sworn, an' a';" an', ere lang, wi' a detachment o' his regiment, the gallant 78th, was on his way to India to join Havelock on his glorious march through an enemy's land, to bring help an' succour to the brave and famishing defenders of the City of Lucknow. Wherever hard work or brave deeds were to be dune on that glorious march, Tam Dalziel was in the midst or front o't, till he became a marked man by the great General. Day by day they were drawing nearer to their destination, till they could maist persuade themsel's they heard the thunder o' the cannon within the beleagured toon.

Ae afternune, after a broiling day, Tam was pacing his silent rounds as sentinel, when, a' at ance, he became aware o' something wriggling like a snake amid the jungle, an', ere

Tam could bring his gun to the " present," there clear'd the open, wi' a spring like a panther, a being mair like a famish'd wolf than a mortal man.

" Who, what are ye ?   Speak, or I'll send this bullet whizzing through yer brain ! "

But afore the man could find words for answer, frae some unseen foe, swift as a flash o' lichtning a licht spear cam' whirling through the air straught to its mark, an' that mark was the heart o' the hunted man.

" That has saved ye frae committing murder," he groan'd ; then, drawing the spear frae the wound, wi' a firm hand held its point for a second or twa atween him an' the licht, he murmur'd mair to himself than his hearer--"This is the en' o' the journey ; the point is poisoned ; God grant me time to speak my message ere it be too late."

Wi' a quick movement he faced Tam.   " Your name ? " he questioned.

" Tam Dalziel."

"Dalziel ! Aye, that was yer mither's name, but nae langer Dalziel but Squire Barton, for I'm Col. Barton, and ye're my ain true son, born in lawful wedlock, an' the last o' the race. When the en' comes, an' that will no be lang, rip open the faulds o' this auld turban an' there ye'll fin' papers, an' deeds, an' yer mither's marriage lines. Pray her to forgie me for the sair wrang I did baith her an' you. Stitched up in this auld waist belt ye'll fin' rupees in plenty to buy yer discharge an' keep yer pouch weel lined till ye gang hame. Thank God, yer mither will yet be the Leddy o' Enterkine Ha', for its a' hers an' yours. Think whiles on yer puir faither, whase worst faut was he had owre muckle siller amang his haun's, an' hadna a heid wise eneuch to guide him in the spending o't. Then, wi' a shiver, that shook him frae heid to fit, like the shaking o' an' aspen leaf, he reel'd an' fell, an' the soul o' Stephen Barton had gone to meet its Maker.

Amang the papers conceal'd in the faulds o' the turban was a closely-written journal o' a' the principal events that had happen'd to him since he had pairted frae his wife. There's nae need to repeat it here word for word, sae, to mak' a lang story short, he tell't hoo Maggie frae the first had been owre shy an' retiring in nature and no hauf showy eneuch to please him. What he wanted was ane wha wad join him in his drucken sprees, an' welcome his loud foul-mouthed companions wi' a smile an' a jest in season or oot it, whenever he choose to bring them hame to finish tleir debauch in his lodgings. This, Maggie, wi' her Godly up-bringing, cudna dae, sae, when a flaunting lood-voiced un-womanly woman cam' across his path, he followed as a bairn wad follow a will-o'-the-wisp, an' she introduced him to her brithers as she said, but wha was in reality her paramour, an unprincipled gambler. Then, when they had fleeced him bare as they thocht, they fled together, but like Nemesis, he followed at their heels and found them at the gambling tables of Monaco playing their old tricks in company. Before a crowded table he struck the villain, and from blows it came to pistol shots, and, in the melee that followed, he shot him down like a dog. To avoid what might follow he took passage in a boat bound for Malta, where, under another name, he became a private soldier. After going to India he had purchased a captain's commission in his own name, soon after being promoted as colonel. Since the breaking-out of the Mutiny he had been taken and kept close prisoner for months, an' noo on his reaching the edge of liberty the end had come thus.

Wrapping him closely up in an auld military cloak they buried him like Sir John Moore "at deid of nicht—the sods wi' their bayonets turning," while inch by inch, nearer an' mair near, crept the vultures o' the desert, waiting for their prey, an' when the men turned, on reaching the camp to tak' a last look they had already begun their gruesome feast, while owre an' abune the taps o' a palm an' bamboo grove on a distant heicht, an' as if watching it a', shone the sweet bricht radiance o' " The Morning Star."

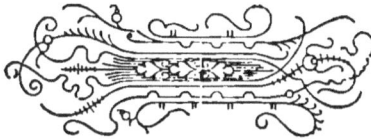

CHAPTER III.

FOR weel on to three years young Tam had been awa' at the weary wars, an' a' the fowk at hame had been breaking their hearts for his sake. For weeks an' months after he had gane awa' there had fawn a hush an' a gloom upon a' things as if there had been a funeral in the hoose. "He'll never come back," droned the bees, as they brush'd their wings against the geranium sprigs on the window-sill, then hurried off in search o' honeysuckles, an' "he'll never come back" the lark seem'd to sing up in the blinding blue. Frae the day o' his landing an' for lang months after, till the peace was proclaimed, his grandfather used to scan owre the list in the papers o' the "killed an' wounded" in an agony o' fear lest his name micht be amang the number. Ance, an' ance only, he had come across his name, an' learned that he had been promoted for some deed o' bravery, an' that was great joy to them. But, noo he was coming home for guid an' a, he had written them, an' ere many months gaed by he wad be amang them again. It was mair than sax months since they had got his cheering letter, an' still he had not returned, when, ae nicht, auld Tam had gane to bed as usual, withoot making ony complaint, but when Maggie opened the shutters in the morning to let in the licht o' a new day she saw the grey shadows o' death had settled doon on her faither's kindly face, an' his speerit, worn oot wi' weary waiting, had gane where "the weary are at rest."

When young Tam steppit oot on the platform at the station on the Brae Tap the nicht after, an' gaed doon the village street, wi' a step as licht as the deer among the heather, in the gray o' the simmer gloaming, he thocht there was something fey aboot the fowk he met. The bairns huddled into entries as he pass'd, an' nane o' the auld familiar faces met him at the corners, but he heard an auld wife, wha had hirpled to the door on her stick to hae a look at him as he pass'd, whisper to hersel', "Eh! preserve us a', there's young Tam Dalziel come back! It wull be a sair hame-gaun for him, puir lad!"

When he got doon the length o' "The Auld Hoose" he noticed the blinds were doon. He opened the front door an' stept into the lobby. Frae a hauf-open'd door he heard the voice o' auld Elder Broon in earnest supplication: "Oh Lord" the voice was saying, "we dinna pray for him wha has gane on afore, as we ken he is safe in Thy keeping, but we do pray for the murning anes wha are left ahint, an' mair especially for him wha is maybe noo oot on Thy great waters. Bring him safe to land, an' may"—but the prayer was never finished, for through the crowd o' neibours wha had gather'd for the "kistin," Tam strode to the coffin side, knelt doon an' kiss'd wi' reverent lips the cauld lips o' the corpse, while he sabbit as if his heart wad break.

"Oh, granfaither, thousands o' miles owre land an' sea I hae come to meet ye, an' this is whaur I find ye."

Some griefs are owre holy for the gaze o' strangers, sae ane by ane the fowk slipit awa' an' left the murners alane wi' their dead.

*   *   *   *   *   *

As sune after the funeral as was becoming, Tam laid the title-deeds afore the lawyers, an' a' things being proved to their satisfaction, afore sax months had gane by they were duly installed as the richtfu' owners o' Enterkine Ha', an' a' things prosper'd they put their hauns to, an' nane grudged the honours that had come sae late to the sweet leddy that had been ken'd amang them a' in her lassie days as "The Morning Star."

Hoo I had a Crack wi' Pharaoh's Son.

AVIE DUNBAR was a character familiar to the
writer when a boy. Davie was a queer yin, an'
got the name o' tellin' big lees; but lees or no, his
stories were aften very queer an' fascinatin'. Aboot
the queerest o' a' Davie's queer stories was ane he ca'd—
" Hoo I had a crack wi' Pharaoh's Son." He had to be gie
near fou afore we got him started to this ane, an' the bauldest
young rascal amang us felt a sweat beginning to rin doon
the sma' o' his back, like a stream o' cauld water, an' his
hair stanin' on en' like the back o' hurcheon afore he had
made muckle progress wi' it.

Davie wad say—Noo, min', ye bairns, this ane I'm gaun
to tell o' is no lauchin' maitter. Min' ye, it's something
that has haunted mysel' since ever it happened, an' to this
day I can mak' neither head nor tail o't,

I wad be aboot aughteen year auld when I gaed to serve

wi' auld Dr Drawbluid, in the toon o' Glentakit, in the
capacity o' coachman, powder monkey, and general factotum.
I had been there aboot three months, when ae afternoon the
Reverend Joshua Windlestrae, the auld anti - Burgher
minister, cam owre to tak' his dinner wi' the Doctor, an' get
himsel' fou as usual. Betty Broon, the Doctor's ae auncient
servant, an' mysel', had been attending to their several wants
for the feck o' the afternune—oot an' in—an' I heard the
twa auld fules aboot aught o'clock, juist awee afore they
pairted, when their heids were mair fou o' wine than wisdom, hae an animated dispute aboot the place that the
Israelites pass'd ower on the memorable morning when they
gaed oot on strike' an' fled afore Pharaoh. The Doctor was
perfectly positive it was through Jordan they gaed, an' the
minister jist as positive that it was through the Red Sea.
At lang an' last, after things had quatened doon awee, I
heard Mr Windlestrae gaun staucherin' awa hame.

After we had got the fragments o' their feast clear'd up
awee, Betty gied me a bit gey stiff dram oot o' the decanter,
an' a platefu' o' rough banes doon wi' me to the kitchen to
pyke ony time afore I tumbled into bed.

I had been enjoying mysel' in this way a guid while,
takin' a bit smoke noo an' then, an' watchin' the antics o'
twa muckle rattons that were sitting up on their hunkers at
different corners, trimming their whiskers, and wunnering
hoo muckle o' my feast o' fat things wad come their wey
when I left aff.

Whether the bit dispute I had heard in the afternoon
aboot the auld Egyptians had onything to do wi' what
happen'd or that I fell asleep and dream'd it is what puzzles
me till this day.

Weel, as I was telling ye, I was sittin' watching the
rattons, when a' at ance I heard frae an auld lumber closet

at the en' o' the lobby, that nane ever ventur'd in, but the
Doctor himsel', a lang wearysome "Och-hech-howe," as if
some ane was yawning an' coming oot o' a long sleep, then
twa lood raps on the back o' the door, an' a queer bass voice
cried oot "Davie! Davie!! Davie!!!" three times, as
distinctly as I'm saying them the noo, an' wi' a soon like
the rowing up o' the wechts o' an auld rusty clock several
times repeated, to save the owner o't the expense o' a
bawbee's worth o' oil. I didna ken hoo it was, but I didna
feel a bit fley'd during the hale interview that follow'd.

"Wha's that," quo' I, "makin' a fule o' themsel's an' me
at this untimeous hour o' the nicht, wha is't ava!" an' I
steppit doon the lobby to the lumber room door an' listened.

"Davie," quo' the voice again, "Davie, my man, slip
awa' up to yer maister's room an' bring doon the key. Ye'll
fin' it at the en' o' his watch cheen. Nae fear o' him seein',
he's faun soon asleep poreing owre a volume o' Dr. Dod-
dridge's Commentary. Bring doon the key, I'm sayin', an'
open this door an' let me oot."

Weel, I did as I was tell't, an' on opening the door there
steppit oot o' an auld wooden box, that was stan'ing up on
its en' against the wa', the queerest looking shaver I had
ever come across in a' my born days. Talk aboot yer
"leevin' skeletons!" I tell ye what, boys, this yin seemed
as if it had been hinging up in the reek o' a lum since the
death o' Abraham. Faulded a' roon' its heid an' chafts
there were as mony plets o' auld yellow cloots as wad hae
made a pair o' blankets. As it was stepping across the
kitchen flure, an' sitting doon cheek-for-chowe wi' me at the
ither side o' the fire, it took them ane by ane aff, an'
drappit them in a heap at the back o' the creepie stule it
had sutten doon on. When the bodie had managed them
a' aff, it lukit across at me wi' its queer een, or, raither nae

een, for the feint haet could I see but a wee weazen'd face o' skin an' bane, no the hauf size o' my haun' a'thegither.

"Noo, Davie, my man," quo' this queer antic, "considering its aboot five or sax thoosan' years, aff an' on, since thae wrappings were aff afore, this is what I ca' real pleasure, an' we can hae a bit smoke an' a crack in comfort.' Licht up yer pipe an' gie's a bit whuff o' yer cuttie."

"But wha are ye ava?" quo' I.

"Weel, then, since ye maun ken, I'm ane o' King Pharaoh's sons, an' when I heard thae twa auld fule fallows haeing their bit dispute ben the parlour the nicht, I had a bit quate lauch to mysel' at their wonnerfu' display o' wisdom. They little thocht there was ane sae near han' could hae gien them a' the oots-an'-ins aboot that Red Sea bizness, for frae a safe distance I saw the hale o't, Davie, my man, at the time it happen'd."

"But hoo did ye manage to wun oor length, Mr M'Pharaoh?" quo' I.

"Hoo did I cum here? Weel, since ye maun ken, I cam' in the carrier's cairt the nicht afore yestreen, an' for the last score o' years an auld blackguard o' a fallow has been hurling me in a rickety waggon roon' the hale kintra side an' makin' a penny show o' me, an' your maister, the doctor, cam' to look at me the ither day, sae I gied him a wink at the time to try an' get me oot o' their han's at a reasonable figure. A bargain was made, an' here I am, richt glad to fin' mysel' in sic comfortable quarters."

"Aweel," quo' I, "it's a lang cry, they say, frae here to Loch Awe, but it's a langer ane frae the noo to the far back days o' the Pharaohs, an' ye maun hae seen mony a queer sicht in yer time, Mr M'Pharaoh."

"Deed have I, Davie, mony a yin. I have min' as weel as if it had been yestreen that afternoon they brocht Moses

into oor hoose, an' ane o' the ootbye workers cam' followin'
up ahint wi' his wee boat made o' seggans. Od I fell in
love wi' his bonnie sister, Miriam, at the first sicht, but
when it cam' to my faither's kening he was sair against it,
an' forbade me the hoose. Sae a' the time the plagues
were making sad havoc through the whole kingdom I was
comparatively safe, for I had taen up my lot wi' the
children o' Israel, an' a' through that wearyfu' nicht when
my auld brither was lying deid up in the Palace I was
makin' ready to flee oot o' the hoose o' bondage wi' them.
We hadna been lang started on oor flicht when I heard my
faither wi' his chariots an' a' his fechting men coming up
close ahint us, an' it was only by a neck we managed to the
ither side o' the Red Sea afore them. My faither, at the
front o' them a', hed got aboot hauf-wey across the water,
an' when on lookin up he saw me safe an' soun' in the
midst o' the Israelites it set him clean delecrit, an' drawing
his bow at a venture, an arrow frae't gaed whizzing an'
crashing through and through my brain ere ever I ken'd
what had happen'd to me, but afore I drappit, I saw him,
my twa brithers, an' their hale following swallow'd up wi'
the great waves, an' horses, chariots, an' men gaun
whaumlin owre an' owre yin anither, an' speedin' oot o'
sicht like a herd o' droon'd stots doon the burns on the tap
o' a Lammas spate. Miriam's sang o' victory was sune
changed to ane o' woe an' wailing when she saw the lad
wha had risked sae muckle for her sake lying deid at her
feet. But they bathed me wi' myrrh, oil, an' spices, an'
rowin' me up in thae swaddling claes ye saw me drap aff
me the noo, they buried me in the first convenient cave
they cam' to in the wilderness. Thousan's o' years maun
hae pass'd owre my heid, when I was wauken'd up ae
mornin' frae my lang sleep wi' the noise o' Napoleon's

armies mairching an' counter-mairching, an' some o' his
generals, baulder than the lave, foun' me in the cave, an'
brocht me oot ance mair into the licht o' day. When the
airmy cam' back to France they brocht me alang wi' them,
an' left me in ane o' their museums, an' there I lay, stared
at by the crowd, for mony a lang day. But the box I had
been laid in, in the hurry o' burying, no haeing sae mony
nick-nacks an' whirly-whas aboot it as some o' the lave that
lay aside me, I was voted oot, an' sel't to the first ane that
made onything like a reasonable offer for me, an' that ane
happen'd to be the auld showman I have already tell'd ye
aboot, an' hoo I cam' here ye ken already. If ye hae ony
doots, Davie, my man, o' the story I've been tellin' ye,
come owre here, an' fin' this hole in my heid—that's whaur
my faither's arrow gaed through."

It's as true as I'm telling ye, boys, I steppit across an'
faun' a hole in his heid ye could hae turn'd yer twa fingers
roon in. I tell ye, I foun't as plain as ye can fin' thae furs
in my new corderoy breeks. Sae I cudna help believing
onything he tell'd me after that, an' we sat an' crackit awa'
aboot mony a queer thing, till at lang an' last he got up
an' says:

"It's getting late noo, Davie, my man; I hear the clock
warning for ane, an' it's owre late for ye to be oot o' bed,
sae ye had better get awa' ti't an' I'll slip aff to mine;
leave the door o' my closet aff the sneck; dinna lock it, I
mean; pit the key o't as quate as ye can on to the doctor's
cheen, he'll never ken whether the place is lockit or no, an'
sae we'll hae mony a crack yet, an' get better acquaint
afore lang, Davie, my man," quo' he, an' wrapping his
cloots roon him again, wi' his heid held as heich as
Gilderoy's, he steppit alang the lobby an' into his closet
juist as the clock was chapping ane.

Juist as I saw him stepping oot o' sicht, I got clean dumfounder'd an' was on the point o' screaming oot, when a' at ance I foun' auld Betty's han' come dingling across my lugs an' her voice shouting in anger—

"What's wrang wi' ye, sir? what's wrang wi' ye the nicht ava, Davie? Here have I been stauning listening to ye at the kitchen door for the last ten minutes' and ye've been daeing naething else but blethering like an auld sweetie wife aboot Napoleon, an' sayin' there was a hole in somebody's heid, an' a hale lot o' ither fule havers; I doot ye've got a guid drap o' smuggled whuskey the nicht conceal'd aboot yer person. Min' ye if the like o' this happens wi' ye again, you young rascal, as sure as your name's Davie Dunbar I'll tell the Doctor aboot it. The clock has chappit ane, the fire's gane oot, an' the cruizie's gaun the same wey, sae if ye dinna want to be left in the dark a'thegither, ye'd better staucher aff to yer bed as quate as ye can, an' be thankfu' ye've won sae easily aff, but dinna daur to dae onything like this again, for if ye dae it's my duty to report ye."

An' I did as she tell't me, but at the first straigh o' day I was alang the lobby an' had a look into the auld closet, but feint haet was there but some auld hats, tippets' an' worn oot riding gear o' the maister's, fit only to be coupit into the rag basket o' the first gather-away that cam' doon oor loaning. An' frae that hour to this I hae never forgather'd again wi' Pharaoh's Son, but often when I'm coming hame some lanely road by mysel', or maybe bringing back James Murray's boar frae some far-off farm in the gloaming, I maist fancy I hear his feet come pitter-pattering ahint, an' fully expect he'll lay his han' on my shoulder some nicht an' salute me wi'—

"Weel, Davie, hoos a' wi' ye?"

"What's that ye've got in yer inside pouch, Pate Telfer.

Ye needna be buttoning yer jacket up ony tichter, my callan; I ken fine what it is, sae for ony sake bring't oot an' let me sook aboot as muckle as wad fill a thimblefu' o't, for whenever I tell that story I fin' a cauld shiver rin through me, an' I maun tak' something hot to keep me frae freezing into an icicle a'thegither."

"Gran' stuff that, Patie, my man; aughtpence a gill if it cost a penny; fin' yer mither kens what's guid for her, but ye'll get Graham's grace an' the psalms o' Comrie when ye gang hame for taigling sae lang on her message. Skirt like lichtning through Bowl Peter's Close, an' if she says onything aboot it being short measure, sae ye poor'd a drap or twa doon an auld man's throat to keep him frae freezing."

O'd, it's a gie cauld nicht, boys, ye'd better creep quately awa hame. As for me, I'm gaun straught up to my bunk o' a bed in the hay laft. Mind ye, boys, a' the stories I tell ye are true anes; if there's ony cratur on this yirth I abhor mair than anither it's a le'er. An' I'm juist gaun to licht the stable lantern ere I drap into bed an' read twa or three pages o' yon auld true story aboot Jack the Giant-Killer, an' ponder awhile owre the first ten verses o' the fifth chapter o' the Acts o' the Apostles.

An' Davie wad hirsel awa frae amang us, while we boys wad daunner hame tae tumble an' toss the feck o' the nicht an' dream queer dreams aboot Pharaoh's son an' the rout o' the Egyptians.

POEMS & STORIES

BY

MRS. JOHN HYSLOP,

KILMARNOCK.

POEMS.

Burns.

AS I sat musing by the fire, soft sleep her mantle cast,
   And soon to my enraptur'd sight rose visions of
      the past;
And then, with Coila by my side, with willing feet I sped,
As long as she would be my guide, to wheresoe'er she led.
" Come first into this peasant's cot, upon the banks of Doon;
Here lies a babe of lowly lot, but who'll be famous soon;"
And then she stoop'd and kissed his brow, and round it
      twined a holly bough;
Then in a voice both loud and clear, summon'd attendants
      to appear,
         Who on this genius wait —

o

And then she asked from each his aid, to endow the babe
    that there was laid,
        And so decide his fate.
Then each and all declared their zeal,
To aid her in the infant's weal,
        Nor further would debate.

Then Honour came and touched the child,
And Hope looked down and sweetly smiled—
While Love breathed words into his ear
To bloom in many an after year;
And Pity touch'd his gentle heart,
And Fancy, too, would act her part—
While Wit would not be kept in bounds
Till roof and rafter all resounds.
Then Independence, Wealth, and Fame,
At his young feet laid down their claim,
To aid him in his coming years,
Tho' fill'd with trials and with tears;

Then Poverty and Sorrow drew
A contrast to the former crew;
They claimed a right to visit there,
As those who wait on Genius rare;
Time said, " He shall in every clime
Be honour'd with a power sublime;
From out the North and Western snow
To where the Orinocco flows;
From Austral's Southern Golden sands
To where the Eastern Empire stands,
In China, Canada, Natal,
Familiar he will be to all;

And every time I turn my glass,
He shall to greater honours pass."
He ceased and silence reigned around,
And I could catch no other sound;
And when I looked, my guide was gone,
And I was left there all alone.

The scene is changed, and years have fled,
While youth and manhood onward sped;
And loves and hopes and cares has he,
While battling with dire poverty;
But still his independence strong,
His love of right and scorn of wrong
Keep him above the turpid wave
That would his every power enslave.
He struggles as it were for life,
He strikes for freedom in the fight,
He sees his brother-man cast down
By tyrants, and he then can frown—
Demands his right with scathing words,
That cut the heart like burning swords.

Hypocrisy he then unmasks,
And, in sarcastic tones, he asks
Some who have got more words than grace,
Whom men think wond'rous clever,
He asks them boldly, to their face—
"To steek their gabs for ever."
And " Holy Willie's " well-worn prayer,
He with his satire strips it bare;
And mourns that any such as he
Would thus disgrace his Majesty —

Who reigns within the " Brunstane" dome,
Where hypocrites must make their home ;
As they exhibit all their shame,
But bring discredit on his name.

I see him now behind the plough,
When the " wee mouse " runs cowering by,
A shadow clouds his manly brow,
And tender pity fills his eye ;
Or the crushed daisy on the lea—
" Wee modest, crimson tipped flo'er,
E'en tho' I mourn ye sair," said he,
To save ye noo's oot o' my po'er.
And then I next beheld a hare
With bleeding breast come limping by,
His malediction men must share,
As he thus sees God's creatures die.

Failings he had, such as each man
Is doom'd to since the world began,
But above each there grew a flower
That bloom'd in sunshine and in shower ;

And how, I thought, in these our days
Shall we withhold our poet's praise :
No ! let the narrow-minded rave
And pass with scorn his honour'd grave,
While they with shaking heads declare,
That all who his opinions share
Are, like him, treading the broad way
That leads to darkness, not to day ;

But we rejoice, and thank our God
That such as Burns our land e'er trod,
And left behind him words to guide
And cheer the widow and the bride,
And teach the faithless how to trust
And cast our good deeds in the dust.
His better nature rising ever,
Till lost within the great forever.

But now my dreams are all disturbed and other voices
call,
And from the arms of balmy sleep I now must surely fall;
And other duties me await, but I've a lesson learned,
And carry with me on life's road a sense of what he earned;
As years revolve, I'll still revere what he has deemed the
right,
His spirit passes ! so I'll bid the poet king good night.

The Heart of Bruce.

HE has fought his last great battle,
  And his bones are laid to rest,
  And a nation duly sorrows
    For the good, the tried, the best ;
By marbled tomb, 'neath sculptur'd dome,
  Full many a tear is shed,
As the Church her rites doth lavish
  O'er her illustrious dead.
The funeral chant now rose, now fell,
  Beneath the massive pile,
While ever and anon's the dirge
  Heard wailing thro' the aisle.
Well may they weep : the day draws near
  They'll seek his like in vain,
For never will old Scotland find
  A king like Bruce again.
But one among his favour'd lords,
  Who knew, who read his life,
And side by side oft swayed his sword
  In thickest of the strife ;
To him the king had spoken thus,
  While yet he own'd his breath,
" My friend, of thee one boon I crave
  When I am cold in death :
When I was often sore beset,
  I vow'd unto my God
Should I see Scottish warfare end,
  I'd leave my native sod,
And forth I'd go, with good intent
  Strike for the truth and right —
Against an unbelieving host
  Be foremost in the fight.

But since my God hath not seen meet
  To grant me my request,
I pray, dear friend, fulfil the vow—
  With you I leave the rest ;
E'en take this heart from out my breast,
  Embalm and thence it bear
Straight to the Saviour's holy tomb,
  And forthwith leave it there.
So fare ye well, my lords, my friends—
  The trusted and the tried."
Thus breathed the Bruce, and so he stretched
  His stalwart limbs and died.

Brave Douglas, on his mission bent,
  Ne'er dreamed of aught but truth ;
But, as in boyish days, he seemed
  To claim a second youth.
He had his master's heart secure
  In silver casket borne,
When, lo ! the warlike Moors appear
  On Spanish field one morn ;
And so he deemed that he might fight
  'Gainst heathen in that land—
He little reck'd how many might
  There meet him hand to hand ;
But with true valour, as his wont,
  He charged the stubborn foe,
And many a haughty Moor he met,
  And laid his proud head low ;
But sore they pressed on every side,
  And Douglas had but few
Who followed him out of the land
  Of Scots—both staunch and true.

But ne'er afraid, nor yet dismay'd,
  The casket he unstrung,
And right into the drifting crew
  The Bruce's heart he flung,
And in a voice above the din
  Each heard the loyal cry—
" Lead on, thou dear, brave, Scottish heart—
  I'll follow thee or die."

Then straight into that sable throng
  His faithful charger bounds,
Close follow'd by each gallant Scot,
  While cheer on cheer resounds.
Alas the day for Douglas now !
  The Moors around him swarm,
Though bravely with his trusted men
  He meets the gathering storm ;
Vast numbers soon o'erpower the Scots,
  Though each fought bold and well,
And with his mission unfulfilled
  The brave Lord Douglas fell.

The faithful knights who had survived
  The bloody onset there
With gentle hands the prostrate form
  They raise with reverent care ;
The precious casket, too, is found
  Near where his body lay.
With bleeding and with aching hearts
  They bear them both away.
And from that land of war and strife

To Scotland they return,
And by his followers—brave and true-
   The Douglas' bones are borne ;

Then, with all pomp and honour due
   To those who fought and bled,
They lay within their own lov'd land
   The relics of the dead.
The heart of Bruce, while living, beat
   For Scotland's good and right,
And Scottish earth alone could claim
   To hide it from our sight :
And now in state it lies enshrined
   'Neath Melrose ancient pile,
And stimulates each noble soul
   Throughout the British isle.
Though ages have rolled on since then,
   Yet daily Scotland mourns
The fall of some good, noble man—
   A Bruce, a Scott, or Burns ;
While honour, truth, and valour make
   A nation's weal the sum
We'll trust to Scottish hands and hearts
   For ages yet to come.

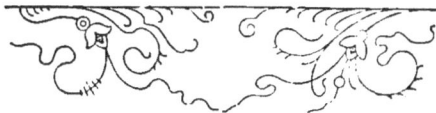

Marion Neville:

A TALE OF WINDSOR IN THE DAYS OF QUEEN MARY OF ENGLAND.

'TIS summer, and green is each old oak tree,
   And verdure clothes the glade,
While the deer bounds graceful o'er vale and lea,
Or idly lying, as one can see,
   'Neath the cool and leafy shade.

The day's work's o'er, and the toilers rest,
   And they gaze with looks serene
On nature tipp'd with a golden crest,
While the sun sinks smiling in the west
   Adds beauty to the scene.

But England's queen heeds naught so bright,
   And no joy can it impart ;
In her eye is the glare of an angry light,
And she welcomes the shade of the coming night
   With a darker shaded heart.

For jealousy there doth sit as queen,
   And rules with an iron rod,
For the days have fled that she hath seen,
And King Phillip's love is no more green
   Which she set in her heart as God.

" Revenge," she muttered, " to me is sweet,"
   Then a golden whistle blew,
But ere she the falcon's cry could repeat
A pale priest entered with noiseless feet,
   And the arras backward threw.

" What wouldst thou, daughter ?" at length he said,
 In his dull and heartless tone,
With voice and look as cold as lead,
And each kind feeling lay wither'd or dead,
 And vice held sway alone.

" Father," the Queen then fiercely cried,
 " Dost bear in mind that day
When I by the holy altar's side
Confess'd and my sinful heart did chide
 Which to evil thoughts gave way ?

" For out from amongst my ladies fair,
 My consort to gratify,
I picked out one with graces rare,
Nor deem'd her beauty might him ensnare,
 And my queenly power defy.

" Then near my person the maid I placed,
 And conferr'd my favours too,
But now the wretch must go forth disgraced
And her memory from my heart effaced,
 And punishment ensue."

" Daughter, these things in my heart I'll store ;
 I fear me 'tis all too true—
E'en now, as I passed King Phillip's door,
A maiden I met in the corridor
 With soft eyes of azure blue

" A creature so fair that the eyes beguil'd,
 With lips of the ruby dye,
With so modest a mien and look so mild
One would think she had been a heaven-born child
 Or an angel standing by."

"What !" shrieked the Queen, "has it gone so far
   That I'll thus insulted be—
That a worthless minion my peace can mar,
And me from my husband's love debar ;
   Good Father, counsel me."

"What counsel doth England's Queen now seek ?
   Is her power not still supreme ?
She hath but to command and show how weak
Are her foes, and on them her vengeance wreak,
   Or a subject's life redeem."

"Ay," saith the Queen, "but it makes me feel
   That it best becometh thee
To deal with her for the Church's weal,
And on her actions to set a seal,
   And thou'lt rewarded be.

"For remember, then," cried the Queen, "I trow
   My power is small at Rome
If a cardinal's hat doth not grace thy brow,
And the living at Hatfield as earnest now
   Of favours yet to come."

"Rest, daughter ! now must thou be content ;
   This night I shall sift the same ;"
And his serpent eyes glowed with ill intent
As he glided through the arras rent
   As noiseless as he came.

Alone again with her thoughts was the Queen,
   And her heart was ill at ease.
But turn from her to another scene,
Where the injured maiden may be seen
   'Neath the spreading forest trees.

And there she stands as a trembling dove
   Is safe in the rocky cleft ;
So she shelter takes in the Powers above,
And closely clings with a heart of love
   To the friends who still are left.

See ! the father hears his daughter's tale,
   While the youth his passions hide,
And, with lips compress'd and cheek more pale,
He inwardly vows he will not fail
   To avenge his insulted bride.

In accents mild the father spake,
   As he kissed his daughter's brow ;
" Be patient, my child, and courage take ;
The Lord will the rod of the tyrant break ;
   To him now in reverence bow."

The torch is lit, and the holy Book
   He takes from its hiding place
'Neath the forest leaves, in a shelter'd nook ;
Then, casting around an anxious look,
   They its sacred pages trace.

The Word of Life to their hearts is balm,
   And they cast away all fear ;
And their voices join in the evening psalm,
Their souls are soothed with a heavenly calm,
   Nor think foes may be near.

But, ah ! too near are the soldiers rude,
   As their prayers to heaven ascend
To the bounteous Father of all good,
In the name of Him whom their surety stood—
   The sinner's greatest Friend.

They are taken and bound and led away,
  As their Master was before,
While the wily priest gloats o'er his prey
As he sees success hath closed his day
  With rewards for him in store.

So before a mock tribunal now
  The intended victims stand ;
No word in defence will their judges allow—
Their doom is seal'd, and they're forced to bow
  To Queen Mary's dread command.

The maiden fair and the man of years
  And the youth in manhood's prime
Meet their fate with faith that subdued their fears,
And darkest doubt, too, disappears
  As they near the bounds of time.

They are soon led forth ; to the stake they're bound ;
  The fatal brand's aflame ;
But why start the crowd and turn around ?
What causeth the horse-hoof and trumpet-sound ?
  'Tis freedom they proclaim.

The captives are free, for the Queen is dead—
  Another is on the throne ;
And their foes shrink back with looks of dread
As the crowds disperse and wider spread,
  And the trio stand alone.

Alone ! not so, for friends are near—
  The host may now be seen ;
The cry, " Elizabeth," meets the ear,
And long and loud rings the British cheer,
  " Long life to England's Queen !"

They are saved ! but seem not yet aware
　　That around is many a friend ;
Like birds escaped from the fowler's snare,
And that life's pleasures they yet can share,
　　They scarce can comprehend.

Their trial's o'er, and, like true gold,
　　From the fire they come more pure,
And their grateful hearts beat with joy untold,
As they cling to their faith with a firmer hold
　　That hath taught them to endure.

Foil'd queen and priest ! foil'd sword and fire !
　　They have borne the tyrant's frown ;
But God in his anger quenched their ire,
While He bids His servants come up higher,
　　And win a conqueror's crown.

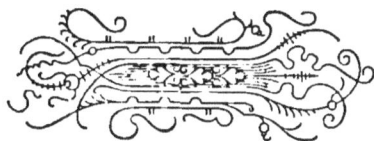

Count Tarset's Trust.

ONE wintry day in olden time, five hundred years ago,
A palmer—weary, old, and grey—came tott'ring
through the snow ;
"'Tis Christmas Eve—a welcome guest," the merry porter
cries ;
"Oh, enter in ! the day wears late, and clouds obscure the
skies."
"My benison be on each soul on whom the sunlight falls—
Either old or young, a special prayer for those within these
walls."
"Oh, welcome art thou, holy man," and Maida took his
hand,
"And three times welcome with the news thou bring'st
from Holy Land.
What hast thou seen, thou palmer grey ? Come, tell us here
and now ;
For well I know thou can't divine what's happened Count
Jefrow ;
With grief we heard that he was dead, my lord so kind and
true,
That he had fallen on Eastern plains, but no one rightly
knew."
"Why dost thou ask, thou lady fair ? for months have
roll'd between
The time that he had left the camp, and hath not since
been seen ;"
"He may be dead," the old man said, "of griefs he had a
store,
And rumour, with her thousand tongues, was always
adding more."

"O, God forbid!" fair Maida cried, "for my betrothed
was he,"

"My kinsman, too," Count Tarset said, "a friend who
cared for me."

The palmer's face grew stern and sad, and chidingly
replied,

"They have proved false, and broken trust, for whom he
would have died ;

So rumour saith, the friend he left hath woo'd and won the
love

Of Maida fair, whom all had thought pure as the heaven
above."

"Go on, go on," Count Tarset said, "what follow'd all
you've told,

No warlike weapon e'er could crush the heart so brave and
bold ; "

But with these tidings he was crush'd, an old man worn
and grey,

He dropped thro' faithlessness of friends, as was seen day
by day ;

And men, it seems, had not been slack, and added guilt to
shame,

And told him that false friends had brought disgrace upon
his name.

"Hold there! hold there?" Count Tarset cried, while
quivered every limb,

"Thou palmer grey, hear this," he said, "I've not been
false to him ;

Should he return I'll yield his bride, pure as the lily fair ;

While in my secret heart of hearts I'll ever shrine her
there.

It is no shame to love a maid, so good, so pure, and true,

And I have not betrayed my trust I plainly tell to you ;"

And, Maida, while the tears roll'd down, dropp'd on her
    bended knee,

"I have been true unto my lord, whate'er he's been to
    me.

But when we heard that he was dead, as friends we did
    confide,

And as we could not bring him back we mourned him side
    by side.

And this thou good and holy man next time thou wilt
    relate

The story of our secret love among the rich and great ; "

That Maida and Count Tarset have been friends both true
    and tried,

And should Count Jefrow e'er return can claim me for his
    bride.

The palmer's guise is cast aside, and there Count Jefrow
    stands :

The master of these courtly halls, and the owner of these
    lands ;

Strange pity stirred his noble soul, and tho' his heart did
    ache,

He'd sacrifice his own desire for this dear loved one's sake ;

While Maida and Count Tarset kneel, and his forgiveness
    seeks,

He roused them up, he kissed each brow, and brokenly he
    speaks,

" I yield my bride to her beloved, the darling of my heart,

As youth and age doth not agree I'll with my treasure
    part ;

And as a warrior worn, I'll rest, while you, my children
    twain,

Will nurse the old man back to health, to strength, and
    youth again ;

And may God's blessing now descend on hearts so tried
    and true,
Be happy in each other's love, and I'll be happy too,"
And so it was that e'er there came another Christmas tide
He, too, rejoiced to see his love the brave Count Tarset's
    bride.

The Sunny Side.

DRAW in yer chair, My ain guidman,
　　And sit ye doon by me,
And a' the hours recount again,
　　We spent in youthfu' glee.

In fancy we'll gang roun' ance mair
　　Each auld familiar scene ;
We'll walk thro' Bellfield's woods sae fair,
　　Or rest us by the Dean.

In thocht we'll hear each croodlin doo,
　　Or merle, or mavis sing ;
And there, guidman, we will renew
　　Oor vows made in life's spring.

When wanderin' doon by Fairy Hill,
　　Whaur Irvine's stream rins wide,
Yer pawky whisper haunts me still—
　　" We'll tak' the sunny side."

That wordie cheered when grief and care
　　Oor youthfu' luiks did mar,
And smoothed oor broos when wrinkled sair
　　Wi' mony an inlaid scar.

Tho' noo oor pows are whitenin' fast,
　　Wi' warly toil and strife,
We hae Hope's anchor aye to cast
　　Thro' a' the storms o' life.

Oor hearts we'll free frae ilka clog,
   Tho' bluid rins thin and cauld;
And blythely to life's end we'll jog,
   Nor mind tho' we grow auld.

Tho' Sorrow's clouds may roon us loom,
   Or death itsel' betide,
Yet we can luik ayont the tomb,
   And " tak' the sunny side."

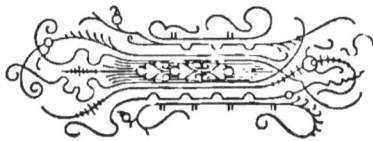

Carlina.

"OH! bairns gie owre yer daffin noo,
　　And no be in yer sport sae keen,
　A tale I'll tell whilk will, I trow,
Bring doon the saut tears frae yer een."
Thus spak oor mither till us a'
　When we were lood in childish games;
She couldna bear us tease or ca'
　Puir auld Carlina tauntin' names.

" Sit doon," she said : " my tale is this :
　Yon puir auld bodie that ye see,
Had been brocht up a braw bien miss,
　A waefu history has she.
Tho' in the warl' we whiles may be
　Wi' a' its guid the heart can crave,
Yet awfu' changes we maun dree
　Atween the cradle and the grave.

" Her faither was a man o' po'er,
　Her mither in her rank taen pride,
Their dochter was the fairest flo'er,
　The gem o' a' the kintra side ;
A gallant captain, young and brave,
　Sae weel did act the wooer's pairt
That in confidin' love she gave
　To him her gentle maiden heart.

" Ae morn in May, when birdies sing
　When nocht can their wee loves divide,
She to his manly airm did cling,
　A blushin' and a happy bride ;

But ah, waes me ! soon war's alairms
    Forced him awa wi' heart richt sair
To lea' his bride in a' her chairms ;
    Perchance he ne'er micht see her mair.

"She mourn'd him sair, puir winsome thing,
    In truth 'twas unco wae to see
Her buoyant smile when hope did spring,
    Or fear brocht tears intil her e'e.
He fill'd her thochts, baith nicht and day,
    Till ance a bonnie bairnie came
That cheer'd her heart, yet aft she'd pray
    Her darlin's faither micht come hame.

" But weel I wat, I'm vex'd to tell
    That hame he never cam' at a',
But on the battle-field he fell
    While vict'ry was within his ca'.
Wi' tremblin' hands a lock o' hair
    He cut wi' his last breath o' life,
And asked his comrades kind to bear
    This last gift to his dearest wife."

" They brocht the news wi' tearless een ;
    She heard the tale they did impart ;
But tho' her grief could no' be seen
    It rent her faithfu' tender heart.
And waur than a' her bairnie dwined,
    And sune awa' to Heaven was taen,
And she was destined noo to find
    That trouble didna come its lane.

"Sae frae that day she nurs'd her grief
    Till it has made her what ye see,
But yet she lives in the belief
    She'll see them baith afore she'll dee.
My story's dune ; yer thochts are stirr'd,
    I see, by thae big tears that start ;
Be kindly, aye! and speak a word
    To soothe Carlina's broken heart."

I'm Far Awa'.

I'M far awa' this Christmas nicht
    Frae joys I weel cud name,
And tho' 'mang freens wi' faces bricht,
    My heart beats aye for hame

I'm whaur the gled New Year comes in
    Wi' sunshine on his broo,
Whaur brichtest flowers and trees are seen
    To bloom the hale year thro'.

And whaur dame Nature dresses gay
    In beauties rich and rare,
Whaur ilka bird its joyous lay
    Sends tirlin' thro' the air.

I'd rather hear wee Robin's sang
    Near frosted window pane,
Or wade the sleety drift amang
    When wreathed on hill and plain ;

Or watch ilk grey and gatherin' clud
    When stormy winter wars
On Carmel's swollen and turpid flood,
    That rows by auld Kilmaurs.

And there to wile an hour wi' Jean,
    Within her mither's cot,
And see love dancin' in her e'en,
    And bless my happy lot.

234

As sune as greedy war's alairms
  A while are cast aside,
I'll come, my love, wi' open airms,
  And claim thee for my bride—

For weel I ken thy faithfu' heart,
  Is fain to welcome me ;
And we will never, never pairt
  Until the day we dee.

Oor Hoose at E'en.

OH what merry times we hae
  In oor hoose at e'en ;
Ilka ane is blythe and gay
  In oor hoose at e'en ;
Tho' the wintry win's may howl,
An' the storm cluds darkly scowl,
An' like angry demons prowl
  Roun' oor hoose at e'en.

When oor guidman comes in
  To oor hoose at e'en,
Tired o' fit wi' drookit skin,
  To oor hoose at e'en ;
See the willin' han's an' feet,
To get in ower faither's seat,
An' for dry claes change the weet,
  In oor hoose at e'en.

Then the cheery cup o' tea
  In oor hoose at e'en,
Maks a' care an' sorrow flee
  Frae oor hoose at e'en ;
Wi' the kindly jokes an' smiles,
An' the bairnies' winsome wiles,
Aye the langest nicht beguiles,
  In oor hoose at e'en ;

Then, wi' hangin' sleepy head,
  In oor hoose at e'en,
Ane an' a' prepare for bed,
  In oor hoose at e'en.

Oh, there's muckle love and bliss,
　Blessings in each darlin's kiss,
E'en their fauts we a' wad miss,
　In oor hoose at e'en.

Then awa' wi' sordid joys
　Frae oor hoose at e'en;
Here there's pleasure that ne'er cloys
　In oor hoose at e'en;
Fain are we it sud be kent
That we're wi' oor lot content,
An' the blessin's Heav'n has sent
　In oor hoose at e'en.

A Hamely Lilt.

Is marriage a failure? Noo, I'm growin' gey auld,
And I needna be blate to be birkie and bauld,
And gie my opinion, an' speak oot my min'—
The truth as I kent it sin' days o' langsyne;
My bonnie Scotch laddie—a fell sonsy chiel—
Sae han'some an' strappin', sae buirdly o' biel,
Had lo'ed me sae weel; was sae couthie an' kin',
I vow'd I wad wed this dear laddie o' mine.

Chorus—

This laddie o' mine, this laddie o' mine,
He aye was sae couthie, sae cantie and kin',
He had a' my heart, sae I made up my min',
I widna keep waiting this laddie o' mine.

And sae we were wedded, an' 'neath oor roof tree
Muckle joy, muckle sorrow we baith were to see;
But oor hearts knit the closer when trials were near,
And love burned brichter an' dried ilka tear;
When the auld canker't carle—Discontent—wad come in,
We just thocht on the joys that were sent frae abune;
Sae I aft used to vow I wad never repine,
Wi' a star aye to guide, like this laddie o' mine.

Chorus

This laddie o' mine, this laddie o' mine,
He aye was sae couthie, sae cantie an' kin',
I vow'd in my heart I wad never repine,
Wi' a star aye to guide like this laddie o' mine.

We've nae gowpens o' gowd, nor acres o' lan',
Nae big hoose or servants are at oor comman';
Oor cot's jist a cosy wee but and a ben,
And my laddie to me is the king amang men;
For my bonnie Scotch laddie has aye been my pride,
Sin' the days that he woo'd me, and made me his bride;
And we're noo just as happy in oor life's decline
As we were at the Clachan in days o' langsyne.

Chorus

This laddie o' mine, this laddie o' mine,
I loe him as weel as in days o' langsyne;
O! wae fa' the day gin the luv I sud tine,
O' this leal-hearted, gray-bearded, laddie o' mine.

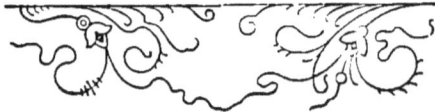

I Canna Gang wi' Thee.

HOO can I ever say farewell
 To you my dainty Nell?
To think that ony ither chiel
 Could win ye but mysel'!
But Oh, my faither, stern and cauld,
 Has vow'd I'll rue't fu' sair,
Gin I persist in bein' sae bauld
 As wed young Nell M'Nair.

But a' his angry threats I'll dree,
 If ye'll the word but say,
And in some bower ayont the sea
 We'll wait a brichter day.
Wi' gowden gear I'll busk ye braw,
 And a' that wealth can gi'e
Will aye be at yer beck and ca'
 If ye'll but gang wi' me.

To lea' my native Scottish hills,
 To lea' my Hieland glen,
To lea' the countless wimplin' rills
 I ne'er micht see again;
To lea' Lochearn's bricht glancin' wave
 And cross the briny sea,
And hide my heid in foreign cave—
 I canna gang wi' thee

Sae noo farewell ! and let me be,
 For here ye ken we pairt,
Yer gowden gems can never gi'e
 The graces o' the heart ;
My Willie is a hamely chiel,
 But Oh ! sae dear to me—
I e'en maun tak' a last farewell
 I canna gang wi' thee.

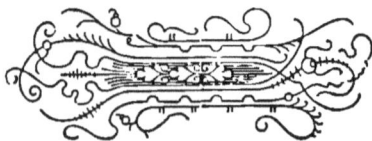

Christabel.

SIR EDGAR the brave has left the plain,
  Where the battle was fought and the victory
    won ;
When the Heathen were routed and many were slain
  'Twixt the hours of the rising and setting sun.

His heart beats high and his hopes are bright,
  As the good ship's steered to his native land ;
And along with many a noble knight
  He waves adieu to the distant strand.

For Sir Edgar loves dearly fair Christabel,
  And his soul thrills with joy as he breathes her name ;
And he sees her smile as she hears him tell
  Of the laurels he's won on the field of fame.

But he asks himself with a growing fear
  If his lady-love would to him prove true ?
And like withering leaves his hopes grew sear
  As he oft the unwelcome picture drew.

But ere he reaches her mansion gates
  He is met by a minstrel hoar and grey,
Who said—" Christabel thy coming awaits,
  And her father swears she must wed this day !

"So give ear, Sir Knight, while to thee I unfold
  Who would win the hand of this lady fair—
He is the Baron of Oswaldwood,
  And he goes by the name of Sir James De Clare !

Q

"Of tainted honour and broken word,
  A kinsman, too, of Sir Edgar the Brave ;
But a brother's blood hath stained his sword,
  And sent thy sire to an early grave !

'Then haste thee, good knight, and ride with speed,
  And cheer the grief-stricken Christabel ;
And this chaplet take as a worthy meed,
  For it yet hath a wondrous tale to tell.

" The crimson stains which the pearls encrust
  Are drops of the blood so foully shed ;
I have kept it here as a sacred trust,
  Till Sir Edgar and fair Christabel should wed.

" Now the time has come, so hie thee away,
  And I shall follow thee ere it be long,
For there is much to be done this day
  To maintain the right and expose the wrong."

Soon this noble youth treads the marble hall,
  And 'mid guests assembled he boldly cried,
And he waved the chaplet before them all :
  " I come to both claim and crown the bride."

Then lightly and quick the young knight laid
  On the lady's head the pearly gem,
While to the Baron he turned and said :
  " How looks my bride with this diadem ? "

" Who," cried the Baron, " dares thus intrude ? "
   As he with rage stood trembling there,
" A son to avenge his father's blood,
   Which imbrued thy hand, Sir James De Clare ! "

" Demon," he shriek'd, as he snatched the pearls—
   But behold the wonder that here befell—
The blood drops down o'er the golden curls
   And the bridal robe of fair Christabel.

And as he stands self-accused there,
   His blade he draws, and with sudden dart
He buries it deep, in his dark despair,
   In the guilty core of his craven heart.

But far away from his lonely grave
   Soon merrily rings each marriage bell ;
'Mong knights there are none like Edgar the Brave,
   No lady so fair as his Christabel.

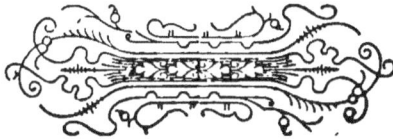

To the Memory of Rev. Robert Kerr, Wakefield, Kansas, U.S.A.

OR hearts are grit and aching sair,
    While tears bedim the e'e ;
  To read the death o' Robert Kerr,
Oor friend ayont the sea.

For he was aye sae dear, sae dear,
    To mony roon' and roon',
But mair to them he aft met here,
    In auld Kilmarnock toon.

We mourn him sair, and sae we weep,
    In spirit owre the grave ;
That hauds him noo in dreamless sleep,
    Ayont the Atlantic's wave.

Nae mair we'll hear his genial voice,
    Or see his kindly smile ;
Nae mair he'll mak' oor hearts rejoice,
    Or weary hours beguile.

'Tis thus we speak ; but 'tis na' true
    We'll hear his voice nae mair ;
We'll aften see, and hear him, too—
    In sermon, poem, and prayer.

His poem on his " Wee Red Rose "
    Lives in each mother's breast,
That had the privilege to lose
    A baby call'd to rest.

He boldly spak' oot for the richt,
    And the oppress'd defend ;
And sae he was held in the licht
    O' ilka puir man's friend.

He tried his sympathy to give,
    Whaure'er the need micht be ;
He tried to teach men hoo to live,
    And teach them hoo to dee.

And tho' he's taen awa' sae sune
    Frae usefu' wark and ways,
We mauna grudge his gowden croon,
    But gie the Maister praise.

Oor natures, selfish, too, and cauld,
    Wad keep amang us still
Ane gather'd to the Shepherd's fauld
    Against the Shepherd's will.

Noo, freen's may grieve baith far an' near
    In weary care and pain ;
The Maister—as he wipes the tear—
    May justly claim his ain.

Dear widowed ane, in lonely grief,
    Amongst thy girls and boys,
God send thee for the gather'd sheaf
    A crap of purest joys.

When earthly skies are clear and bricht,
    Faith's vision oft grows dim ;
God shadows sends ; then comes the nicht,
    To bring us nearer Him.

STORIES.

The Face at the Window.

A GHOST STORY.

CHAPTER I.

"ARE you all ready, bairns?" said my grandfather to us, as a dozen eager, expectant faces looked up into his, one Christmas night, and each one trying to get as close to him as possible.

We were all expecting to hear something very weird and terrible, but not a bit less anxious to hear it related for all that. Grandfather had promised to tell us a ghost story of his own experience if we waited till Christmas, and now the time had come; and as we with one voice answered "yes" to his question, he began. I will try and give the story in his own words.

"It's a lang while noo sin' the time I'm gaun to tell ye o'. I was then a buirdly young chiel' o' twa-and-twenty or there-aboot, and I leeved wi' my faither and mither at a fairm ca'ed Darochside, aboot sax miles frae Crieff. A braw fairm it was, atweel, wi' three pair o' horse, and mair than a dizzen kye, land that bore aye a guid crap and paid weel. I bein' an only bairn had mony advantiges that didna fa' tae the lot o' every son o' the soil. I was better educated than mony, or, at least, I oucht to be, for muckle siller was waured on me and naething hained that wad be for my guid. I was alloo'd a little pocket money, but a very sma' share, as my faither held steively to the principle o' never spendin' a shillin' whaur he cud save ane, and, besides, he didna see that a laddie like mysel' needed muckle siller. Weel, to do mysel' justice, I didna grumble at this, for I weel kent I had every comfort their kind hearts cud bestow, even to my companion and playmate—my bonnie cousin, Katie, my mither's youngest sister's dochter—a sweet bit lassie. Atweel, her parents deein when she was a wee bairn, my faither and mither adopted her and she became their dochter in very truth, and was beloved as if she had been their very ain. To me, after my faither and mither, Katie was a'thing even in thae early days, and tho' a sturdy laddie o' eight years, when laddies like to get a' their ain way, I lo'ed my wee cousin owre weel to dispute a wish wi' her. She aye got the first and best o' a' I had, and naething was richt if Katie didna get her share o't.

Sae thus we grew up, Katie in her sweet childish way returning my devotion by every little kindness her gentle heart cud invent. Weel, aboot the time she was auchteen year auld she was as braw and bonnie a lass as one cud hae set een on, besides she was clever and weel educated and trained in a' the ways o' thrifty hoosekeepin'. My mither watched wi' muckle pride the growth o' her talents and the development o' her mental faculties, and the anxiety she showed to tak' the burden aff her shoothers on till her ain. I mysel' began to look on my cousin in a different licht. I saw new beauties springin' up in her ilka day, and felt kin' o' queer when I spak' to her. She didna seem to be the same lassie at a', but that an angel had got on Katie's claes and had taen her place. I cudna help frae thinkin' o' her at my wark or dreaming aboot her when I was sleepin'; and mony a time, when I sud be squaring up accounts and sic like, I wud start up frae my reverie to find I had wasted a hale oor or mair at a time. I cud hae worshipped the grund she trod on, and yet I never questioned my heart as to the cause o' a' these strange feelin's. I was happy as lang as I cud be near her, never jalousin that ither een had opened to her charms as weel as mine, but I had sune to fin' that oot. It happen'd this way—oor neebor fairmer, John Burton, was the first in a' Strathearn to hae his fields clear o' the hairst crap, an', as was customary, there was to be a grand Harvest Home, or Kirn, as it was then ca'ed. A' the fairmers in the district had been invited, and as mony friends as would care to come. Weel, there was mony a braw lad and mony a sonsy weel-faured lass, servant men, and servant maids ilk ane wi' their Jo, as weel as the sons and dochters o' a' the resident fairmers; but no ane cud come up to my cousin, sae I thocht, for I had nae een but for her, and I, like a fule, thocht that she leeved for me alane. I had juist risen to lead her aff to a kintra dance when I seen she had gotten in tow with Mr Burton's son, Willie, and they seemed sae happy crackin' awa' to ane anither that my heart gaed a great stoon, and I stachered back to my seat, sayin' to mysel' what a fule I hae been no to think o' this afore; I micht hae kent some ane wad step in afore me,

and then— if I lose her! O! then if I lose her! I kent
the fun for me was owre that nicht.

Willie Burton convoyed us hame, to my great annoyance,
and as he bade us guid nicht, he said, in rather a forward
manner, (to my thinkin') to Katie, 'Ill be owre to see ye the
morn's nicht.' He never even speired her if he micht
come. Of course a sense o' propriety kept me kind of
ceevil till him, tho' the fire of jealousy was eatin' my very
heart oot, and I said, in as freenly a way as I cud, (for Katie
didna speak) " We'll be a' gled to see ye, Willie,' but I felt
mysel' tremlin' as I said it, and wonner't if he wud ken
by my words that I for ane didna want him. Katie and I
gaed into the hoose thegither, but scarcely ae word was
spoken. She kent I wasna ower weel pleased at Willie's
proposal. We were a' crackin' neist day o' the gran' daein'
at Burton's, and I happened to say in a half joke, hale
earnest, banterin' way, that Willie Burton seemed fair on
for Katie, when my mither luckit at me in sic a way as I
canna forget, and said—"Willie Burton get oor Katie;
na, na, as lang as I can prevent it. He's maybe a nice
eneuch lad and strappin' eneuch, but his manners are no
mendin' of late. Na, na, Katie, dinna let yer love licht
there if yer wise; he's nae match for ye at a' my lassie."
Katie blushed and hung her heid, but didna answer. Then
says I, " Surely, mither, yer no expectin' Katie to get the
laird, or some braw man oot o' her station in life, wha'll tack
her frae us a'thegither, and we'll ne'er be able to come near
her again!" "There's mony a laird and lord, aye, and
duke, that's nae match for her, and I'll try and keep her
as lang as I can aside me, Robin; what say ye to that, my
doo?" She turned roon for the expected answer, but Katie
had slippit awa, her bonnie een filled wi' tears--a sure sign
that young Burton was the favoured ane. Sae I thocht.

"Tho' I cudna be cauld to my cousin I studied sair to curb my feelin's and to be on sisterly terms wi' her, but I began to look on Burton with aversion amountin' to hatred. His visits to Darochside were maist distastefu' to me, but I reasoned to mysel' that it was no affair of mine if Katie chose him instead of me, forgetting that I had never asked Katie to even try to care for me, or told her the state o' my heart; but the time was comin' sune when I was to ken my fate."

"As I feel a wee tired, I'll rest a while and begin again."

"But, grandfather, did she marry Burton?" cried one with childish curiosity, while others cried out, "What about the ghost?" and so on till poor grandfather had to put his hands on his ears and call us all to order. "A' in guid time noo, a' in guid time, my bairns; I'll sune begin again, if ye'll sit quate and let me tak' a snuff."

CHAPTER II.

DURING the fifteen or twenty minutes that elapsed before grandfather resumed his story we thought it an age, although cake and fruit were handed to each of us; between whispered speculations as to the probable result of gran'pa's love-making and the shuffling of little feet forced him to begin again. "There's never a ghost in it yet," grumbled one little fellow. "Perhaps Katie is going to die and her ghost comes to see grandpa," said Minnie. "You wont let me be put to bed till I hear the finish of the ghost," said little Johnnie Green. This last appeal was sufficient. "No, Johnnie, sit ye doon, my dear; I'll juist tak' anither pinch, and then, Johnnie lad, I'll begin." All was silence, and grandfather went on—

"Weel, I said the time was comin' when I was to ken my fate, and wha Katie lo'ed, and wha she wished to marry. It was ae day when I cam' back frae Crieff, bein' sent there by my faither alang wi' twa o' the lads wi' twa lade o' corn to Crieff market—Thursday bein' the market day and I had to do business in my faither's stead, and it the end o' November I was to sell the corn and gee orders for a miscellaneous supply of necessary guids that were likely to be needed in the hoose for a time, as it wasna ilka day the cairts were in the toon. Ane o' the cairts was laden wi' coals, while the guids were packed into the ither cairt—eneuch to ser's till my mither and Katie wad gang to mak' their purchases in view o' New Year and Hansel Monday, as Hansel Monday was the chief day amang the kintra foulk at that time. Sae as I had a guid harle o' things to get, an' a lot o' gates to gang, it was afternune afore I got started for hame, and the day bein' at the end o' the year it was sune dark, and when I cam' to the lane I had to pick my steps, as the road was heavy and slushy. It was sax o'clock, and as I was kind o' tired I was takin' my time gaun in the lane when I heard the front door slammin' to, an unusual thing, unless there were strangers aboot. Weel, I waited and watched the garden yett to see wha was there. In less than a minute I saw the figure of a man come oot, and come up the lane meeting me. He didna seem to see me, and I said in a cheery voice, 'Fine nicht, freen," but I got nae answer, and I wunner't wha it cud be, sae I gaed in by the back door and was welcomed by Katie as weel as her fluster'd manner wad alloo, but I guessed she was put aboot, but I taen nae notice—I merely speired whaur was a' the foulk. She said my faither had gane to John Bain's for a crack, and my mither had gane to visit Mrs. Stalker, wha had been ill for a guid while, and my faither was gaun roon that way to bring her hame.

"Hae ye gotten a' the things in, Katie," I speired.

"O, aye, I think I've gotten a' thing. Tam carried them in, and I coonted them ; there were aughteen parcels a'thegither."

"Hoot, awa'," says I, "there maun be mair than that." Sae sayin', I gaed to the stable whaur the lads were sortin' their horses, and foun' that the saip box, and a sma' barrel

o' herrin', and some twa three mair things, were to bring
in, sae I telt the chaps to fetch them after they were dune
wi' their horses.

"Did ye see ony stranger when ye were in," I speired at
Tam.

"Aye, Will Burton was in, and he seemed awfu' angry,
and sayin' something to Katie about that she wad rue it.
I didna hear the drift o' onything, though I micht, for he
was speakin' lood eneuch, but I kent I had nae business
wi' ither foulks affairs. I saw Katie was sair put aboot,
for she was near greetin'."

"Weel, ye'll tak' in the rest o' the things when yer ready,
and get yer supper, Rab and you, for ye'll be tired like
mysel'. I'll awa' to the hoose." Sae sayin', I crossed the
coort, for I was baith tired and hungry, but ere I got to
the kitchen door I heard an awfu' screich. I kent it was
Katie's voice, and hurried ben to the parlour, where my
supper was waitin' me. Katie was sittin' in an arm chair,
as white as a cloot, and scarcely able to speak.

"Oh, Robin, Robin," she cried, "it's awfu' gruesome; save
me, Robin. It's maybe only a trick he's wantin' to play on
me."

"Wha's wantin'? What is it, Katie? What's wrang?
Tell me, ye ken I loo ye owre weel to let oucht happen ye.
What is it? Tell me, Katie."

"Oh! the face at the window," she said, and she gave a
frichtit look owre til't, an' wi' a piercin' scream she fented
clean awa'.

By this time the lads had come in frae the stable, and the
lasses frae the byre, where they had been milkin' the kye,
they a' cam' runnin' ben to see what was the maitter.

"Water," I cried, "she has fented."

It was quickly brocht, and we bathed her face and

hands, but it was a lang time ere she cam' roon. I was
ower muckle put aboot to think o' enquirin' into the cause.
At last we had the satisfaction o' seein' her open her een,
and I taen doon the brandy bottle that was kept sacred for
an emergency like this, and I made her swallow a drap o't.
She sune was able to tell what she had seen at the window,
or at least describe it. Sae I'll just gie ye her ain words.

"Oh, Robin, I canna gie ye a' the particulars. I saw sic
an awfu', gruesome face—o' a blae white wi' awfu' starin'
een and —and," here the puir thing begood to sob again as if
her heart wad break.

"Oh, Katie, quo' I, ye've just been feeling lanely, a'body
bein' awa' the day, and you were maybe thinkin o' some
ghaist story ye've heard; besides there are sic things as
optical illusions—ye're nervous, Katie, juist lettin' yer fancy
rin." I was cut short by Katie saying—

"Na, na, Robin, I'm no a cooard, and I was richt busy
a' day and had nae time for thocht o' ony kind but o' my
wark. I was sae taen I loukit twice afore I cried oot, but
I was sayin' the face was o' a blae-white, and a' the broo,
and ane o' his cheeks was a' smeared wi' something, either
wi' bluid or glaur, as if he had fa'en and cut himsel."

"Some drucken gangrel body nae doot," quo' I.

"Na, he wasna like a gangrel, for he had on a white shirt
and white waistcoat, but he had nae hat, and baith the
shirt and vest were a' stroked wi' something juist as if he
had fa'en in some dub or on a cairn o' stanes and cut
himsel', and he was sae white and ill luikin' that I cudna
help screechin."

"Nae wonner, Katie,' quo' I; the puir cratur may be
aboot the garden yet; maybe fainted for ocht we ken. I'll
tak' a turn wi' the lads and see, while Jeanie and Maggie
will bide wi' you. A pity to think o' a fellow-cratur

sufferin' and no lend a helpin'-hand if he's aboot. I'll shut the shutters and the licht 'll no attract ony mischievous loon that micht chance to gang by the lane heid. We'll see if there's ony marks o' fitsteps ootside the window afore we gang ony farrer."

" But ye'll tak' yer supper first, Robin, and let the lads get their's."

"Na, na, Katie, I cudna eat a bite till I ken something mair aboot that puir body," for tho' Katie tried to be calm I cud see she was gey feart to let me gang frae her side, and I didna wonner at it ; for there was aye some faith in ghosts, or apparitions, spunkies and sic like, and, man tho' I was, I felt a cauld shiver run thro' me, tho' for her sake I spak' as lichtly as I cud aboot what she had seen. I got the twa lads and wi' a lantern we gaed oot and examined the grund ootside the window. Sure eneuch there were fit-prints o' a gey bit fit, and even tracked them to the edge o' the gravel walk, aside the yett, and oot to the lane, but instead o' gaun oot the lane they seemed to turn in thro' the coort, and we then made sure that the visitor, whae'er he micht be, was still aboot, sae we searched ilka place baith oot and in we cud think o', but naebody was there. We then cam' to the conclusion that the body was drunk and had stachered awa' hame, sae we gaed back to the hoose and found the lassies composed but wearyin' for us to come in. When we reported oor suspicions they begood to be something like themselves again, and even lauched at the silliness o' their fears (for the ither twa were as feart as Katie, only they didna see the object). While we were takin' oor supper aboot nine o'clock the auld foulk cam' hame and Katie's ghost was the subject o' conversation, when my mither exclaimed—

" I see it a' noo! I was up at Stanninfauld and Mrs.

Tamson telt me that the auld doctor frae Muthil was there afore I gaed in and that he luikit unco queer like. She first thocht he was drunk, but he was sae white and ill luikin' that she speir'd if he wad tak' a taste o' spirits, but he shook his heid, and said, no. He said he was passin' and that he ca'ed in to see if she had any razors o' Mr Tamson's and he thocht that she michtna need them noo that he's awa, and as he kent John keepit a guid lot he wad hae a chance o' gettin' a guid ane."

" Weel, doctor," quo' she, " I had sic things, but as they were nae use tae me after puir John's death, I cudna bear to see them, nor his claes, and I gae them a' to his brither, George, at Grangeton, but," quo' Mrs Tamson, " suppose I had a dizzen in the hoose I wudna gi'en him ane the nicht, for he was like as if there was something far wrang wi' him."

" It wad juist be him, puir saul, and he maybe had fa'en, but we'll hear richt aboot it the morn."

" And sae we a' did, for ane o' oor lads had been at Woodside fairm wi' a pair o' hens, we had the len' o', and cam' rinnin' in, white and breathless, and telt us that they were carryin' in the corpse o' auld Doctor Douglas when he went 'yont, and it was covered up in the cairt shed, and that Mr Dalgleish, the maister, was oot o' ae fent into anither. My faither and I waited to hear nae mair, but set aff to see for oorselves. It was owre true, and sic a sicht I cud ne'er forget sud I leeve to the age o' Methuselah. He had taen awa' his ain life in a determined manner ; seven broken lances were lyin' beside him, and ane stickin' in his neck when they found him : his face, shirt, and waistcoat were a' bespattered with bluid, juist as Katie had seen him. It seems he had began to guddle at himsel' wi' the lances when he cudna get his hands on a razor. He had commenced his deadly wark afore Katie had seen the face at the window. He waunered sine till he got near Woodside fairm hoose whaur he finished the wark he had begun aside a cairn o' stanes."

" In the early mornin' afore it was clear daylicht, while lookin' for twa ewes in the muir, Mr. Dalgleish cam' on the body, and being a man in weak health, very near lost his own life owre it. After makin' his way back to the hoose he startled his wife and family sair by saying there was somebody lyin' deid oot at the cairn, then sank in a chair and fainted clean awa. It cast a gloom owre a' the kintra side whaur he was kent, for a' body liket the auld doctor, and naething short o' insanity cud hae been the maiter wi him when he committed sic a deed."

" I maun stop noo for a wee and get a snuff ; ye maun get an apple apiece for behavin' sae weel."

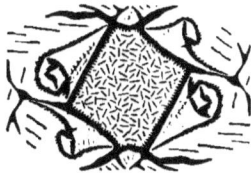

CHAPTER III.

WE were all quiet enough during the interval, and tho' we elder ones were eager enough to hear the end, we were awed into silence by grandfather's story. Each seemed to be afraid of the sound of his or her own voice, and not a question was asked. He saw the effect his story had on us, and he said cheerily, "ye'll hear what silly foulk are in the warl' and hoo the ghaist story is raised and believed in too. Weel, as sune as I got an opportunity I spiered at Katie what angered Burton at her and what he was daein there the market nicht, but she was sweer to gie me an answer, and said he juist ca'd in on the byegaun. But what angered him, I spiered."

"Hoo dae ye ken he was angry or that he was here at a' for that pairt o't?" quo' she.

"I ken weel eneuch," quo' I, "for I met him in the loan as I cam' doon. I spak' to him but I got nae answer, sae I thocht there was something up wi' him." I didna tell her I got my information frae Tam or that it was sae dark as to be uncertain o' the identity o' the chiel I spak' to.

"It was a queer like thing to get angry at you, Katie, the ane he seems sae ta'en up wi'; what was he sayin'? if it's a fair question; ye ken I'm yer brother as weel as yer cousin, and what troubles you troubles me."

"He brocht me a caird to gang to a grand dinner the week after neist, and I wadna tak' it, and then he begood sayin' things that I wudna listen till and " ——

"And what, Katie?" quo' I.

"Juist things he had nae business to say to me, for I dinna care a strae for him, and I telt him sae."

"Makin' love to you and sic like, eh, Katie? I thocht ye cared a heep for him," quo' I, probin' her, and I felt my heart loupin' for joy for I kent I had yet a chance. "I'm sure he's a nice eneuch sort o' chiel," quo' I; "mony a lass wad snap at him."

"Ay, I daursay, but mony a lass is no Katie Wother-spoon" quo' she, and her voice tremmelt. "If I canna get the lad I like I'll hae nane."

"But wha dae ye like, Katie? Ony ane, I'm sure, micht be prood to get my bonnie cuisin."

"I'm no gaun to tell you that. I'll try, as Burns says, and keep something to mysel," she said saucily.

"Ye'r quite richt there," quo' I. "But what if I guess? Will ye tell me then?"

"That depends—but ye'r unco curious the nicht to ken what disna concern ye, Robin," and she hung her heid to hide the blushes that was fast risin' to the roots o' her hair.

"But it does concern me, Katie, and I ken ye care for me, sae ye needna say anither word. I care for you ony-way, and nae ither woman will ever be my wife if I dinna get you," and I steppit forrit and ta'en baith her hands and said—"Noo, Katie, juist luik me in the face and say ye dinna care for me." She raised her bonnie blue een filled wi' tears, her face crimson, and said—"I canna, Robin, I canna say that. I care mair for ye than for a' the warld beside."

"I clasped her to my heart and told her she was a' the

warld to me, and mony a sweet word I said to her, and
mony a lovin' name I ca'ed her, until she lukit up again
and spiered if I wasna gaun owre far, for she didna think
it lukit like a very fervent wooer to stand by and let young
Burton step in afore me. I cudna say ocht else than that
I thocht she cared for him, whilk indeed was the truth.
Noo that I was sure o' her love I was as happy a man as
was in the hale kintra side ; and when the auld folks cam'
to ken o' oor engagement they were overjoyed, and had a
grand pairty to celebrate the event, friends and neighbours
bein' invited. Weel, this was close on Christmas, and the
Dalgleish's were to hae a gatherin' o' young folk on
Hogmanay-nicht, nae elders bein' bidden owin' to Mr.
Dalgleish bein' a guid deal shaken after the auld doctor's
death, and it was thocht advisable to keep him as quate as
possible. Willie Burton was among the lave, and tho' I
jaloused he was up to some mischief he was very cecvil to
baith Katie and mysel'. He danced and joked wi' her, but
I wasna a bit jealous noo--for a' body kent that Katie and
I were to get marrit as sune as arrangements were made
aboot the fairm o' Dargel, aboot twa miles frae the auld
foulk, atween Crieff and Muthil, sae ilka thing seemed to
favour us sae far. Hoo little we thocht what a silly freak
would cost us."

"The pairty brak up aboot three o'clock i' the mornin', but
Katie wished to gang hame atween ane and twa, sae she
intimated her intentions and was sair prig'd to bide, but as
she promised my mither, wha wasna very weel, she wud gang
hame."

"Willie Burton heard her stating the time she was to
leave, and I noticed he had disappeared a while afore we
left, for of course I was to gang hame too. Weel, we had
juist crossed the burn and turned roon the corner o' the

wood leadin' doon to oor ain hame, we were switherin' whether to cross the park or gang roon the road ; hooever, it bein' moonlicht we decided to cross the park, it bein' the nearest, and we were gaun forit to the yett to open it, when frae ahint the dyke, close to the yett, raised a figure very slowly with ootstretched hands and a face death-like in its whiteness, and, to a' appearance, the face and claes a' bedabbled wi' bluid. Katie gaed ae screech sic as I'll never forget and fell senseless at my feet. I was bewildered, for this was an exact coonterpairt o' Katie's description o' the face at the window, and I had an awesome fear the spirit o' the auld doctor had re-visited the earth—but it was only for a minute—and wi' a spring I was owre the dyke, and raisin' my heavy staff, cried ' be ye man or deevil I'll try yer mettle,' and cam' doon wi' a crashin' blow on the bare heid o' the wud-be ghaist ; he staggered and fell wi' a groan. I saw the bluid rinnin' doon below the wig he had on. I looted doon and raised his heid, and wha sud it be but Willie Burton. He had played oot his threat to puir Katie, but he paid weel for his fun. What was to be dune ? I left him, and liftin' Katie in my airms I hurried hame, for she was still unconscious. I was gettin' feart there micht be twa deaths afore I cud get help. I roused the hoose, and leevin' Katie to the care of my mither and the twa lassies, I got my faither and Rab Neilson to help me doon haste for Dr Tait, frae Crieff. Burton remained unconscious, but by the time the doctor came Katie was raivin' in delirium, pointin' and tellin' us a' to luik at the face at the window. The doctor said that she was in for a severe attack o' brain fever, which proved to be owre true. For weeks she lay tossin' and strugglin' atween life and death till we a' thocht she had lost her reason, but at last the crisis came, and thro' the goodness of a kind Providence she began slowly to mend, but it was lang afore she cud comprehend what had befa'en her."

"Willie Burton's case wasna so serious as was at first imagined ; he had got an awfu' smash, that to a weaker man micht hae been serious, but wi' carefu' nursin', at the end o' a fortnicht he was able to be removed to his ain hame. His mother, wha was wi' him a' the time, expressed the hope that the trouble he brocht on himsel' wud gie him a settlin (for be't understood naebody laid ony blame at my door for the clure he got); moreover, Mrs Burton often cam' and helped my mother to nurse Katie till she was oot o' danger."

"Sae spring glided into summer and a' fears for my cuisin were at an end, tho' she was still pale and very douce, but we sune had the satisfaction o' seein the roses bloomin on her cheeks and heard her happy laugh ance mair, and as Christmas drew near a' things seemed to richt themselves—for we were speakin' ance mair o' biggin' a nest. And in due time things were in workin' order—the fairm stocked and a' the weddin' braws bocht and made. Oor waddin' was to be on Hogmanay ; mony were bidden frae far and near, and we slippit into oor new life's wi' the best wishes o' a' concerned in the story, for even Willie Burton did a' in his poo'er to further oor happiness, nor did he leeve in single blessedness, for he taen for his bride bonnie Mary Sharp, a neebor fairmer's dochter ; they were frequent visitors and among oor staunchest freens, but whenever onything happens to refer to that awfu' nicht, Willie looks very grave and says it was the makin' him, tho' it was dearly bocht."

"Noo, bairns, I'm dune ; when ye hear o' ghaists be sure there's a real backin' to a' sic stories juist as there was ane to the ane I've telt ye, 'The Face at the Window.'"

In Foul and Fair Weather.

A STORY OF KILMARNOCK.

"SANDY, Sandy! yer an auld haverel, to think ye wad come to me for ane o' my kitchen towels or guid dusters to dicht the auld mare's face or her harness either; ane wad think ye were gaun to drive Miss Alice to her bridal instead o' lettin' her doon at the station for her lang journey. Puir lassie; I'm wae to pairt wi' her, but ye see there's nae help for't."

"Deed, ye may weel say that, Isie, woman; juist as wae to pairt wi' her as if she was my ain bairn. Kennin' her as I ha'e dune since ever she saw the licht, I feel a sair stoon' gaun thro' my heart when I think I may never see her again, for I'm an auld man noo, an' it may be years afore she comes back frae India—if e'er she does come back. I aften won'er hoo oor hearts get sae boun' up in foulk wha's nae sib till us."

"'Deed, that's a mystery to mysel', Sandy; but here's yer cloot. I maun see that the lunch is ready in time, an' that it's richt, as it's her hindmost for a while, at onyrate, in this hoose." So saying, Isie turned to resume her duties in the kitchen, while Sandy went thoughtfully back to the stable to dress Maggie, as he called his old favourite mare.

The subject of the above colloquy was a Miss Alice Moreland, a young and very prepossessing girl, the niece of a wealthy and much respected business gentleman in Kilmarnock.

Born in India, where her father's regiment had been stationed for a number of years, she had been sent home to receive the advantages of a British education, as seminaries were not so plentiful in the great Eastern Empire then as they are now. Her school days being over, she was to return to India. Her mother, now a widow, visiting her friends in Scotland a few months after the death of Colonel Moreland, was to return to India, as her only son, Harry, held the post of Lieutenant in the Bengal Cavalry. They were to sail from London by the "Euripides" one week later than the date of the commencement of our story, and their departure from Kilmarnock could now brook of no delay.

Great was the grief and many the protestations of love and lasting friendship between the relatives at Irvineside Villa, the residence of George Melville, Esq., Alice Moreland's uncle, but no one seemed so depressed at the parting as Mr Melville's eldest son, Arthur. He seemed to keep apart and dread the parting with his fair cousin so much that it appeared in the eyes of some of his friends to border on indifference. But not so, for Arthur loved his cousin Alice as some only can love and that once in a lifetime, yet his love was unspoken, and he thought to himself he had no right to fetter Alice by expressions of attachment that might issue in pain to both. He knew he could not offer Alice a home for some time to come, he being only twenty-two years of age, and holding not a very lucrative office in a bank in town.

Prospects were good. However, time and hard work alone could lead him to the height at which his ambition aimed, and he determined to gain it. How he succeeded the sequel will show.

" Drive up the carriage for the ladies, Sandy," said Mr Melville, " and Arthur and I will go down to my office, and we will meet you all at the station by two o'clock."

" I'se dae that, sir ; but beggin' yer pardon, I'm sair put aboot this day. I had aye a houp that Miss Alice wad bide wi' us, but I've been mista'en. God bless and prosper the dear cratur whaure'er she may gang," and his voice shook, while his honest old eyes filled with tears.

"Thank you, Sandy ; I know you wish her well, and us all ; but we must part for a while. We may meet again after a year or two, if it please God."

" Ay, sir, and it wad be the prood and happy day for me sud I leeve to see't ; but I'm gey far agee, if I dinna hae trouble, and muckle o't, afore lang."

" Oh, Sandy ! there is no time to-day for prognostics, so just as soon as you're ready drive round and I'll meet you all at the station."

" I'll be in time, sir, depend on't," and Sandy, who was as true to the minute as the needle is to the pole, turned to give the finishing touches to his toilet and to harness the horses to the carriage.

Sandy was one of those men who make their master's interest their own, and often what only gladdens or saddens the hearts of their employers makes theirs to run over either with joy or sorrow, as the case may be. And in truth such do exist, or it would be sometimes a sorry world to live in.

On the present occasion Sandy himself could not account for the depression that took hold of him, and though he knew that Mrs Moreland and her daughter were to be taken care of by a special friend of the late Colonel Moreland, he told himself over and over, "That he did not like him; there was aye a something aboot him that made his heart grue," an expression he seldom used except he had some special dislike or ill-feeling towards the parties concerned, as was the case on the present occasion. He wondered at himself for being sae dead set at this man. "His manners are polished," reflected Sandy, "but I'm sair mista'en if I dinna ken him. I could lay my head that it's that fellow Grantly that used to come to Colonel Moreland's quarters when we were stationed at Aberdeen, afore he started for India. I'm sure it's him, though the years ha'e made a difference, baith on him an' me—I really believe it was ordained for me to come here twa years syne to uncover the rascal, an' I'll dae't; ay, I'll dae't. He has a' the kiks o' a fine gentleman, and can draw the blinders owre the een o' a' the foulk he wants tae ca' his frien's. Aweel, let him be wha he likes, e'en though he was the verra deil, he'll no get a hair farrer than his tether. If I could get but a word o' Miss Alice, I wad gi'e her a bit hint like to put her on her guard, for there's evil brewin', an' nae mistake; but I'll keep my een open while I can, an' warn them to keep theirs—but losh me, what am I haverin' at; I thocht I was ootward boun', as I was wi' the Colonel years syne. But na, I maun e'en bide here an' lippen to Providence, and the richt 'll come the richt way after a'."

So reflecting, Sandy hurriedly looked his watch, and seeing his time was almost up, as fast as his old limbs would allow him, got up on the box, and with his watchword—"Come, Maggie," was soon at the hall door of Irvineside Villa.

Miss Moreland, with a sorrowful heart and tear-bedimmed eyes, bade all the servants farewell, after leaving a little keepsake with each, tho' there was little need of anything to remind them of her or keep her memory green in their hearts, for she was greatly beloved by all, and especially by old Sandy, who contrived to say a word of caution about their escort, Grantly, not altogether flattering to that gentleman's good name, and the response of Alice showed but little trust in him for all his blandishments. Her mother, however, was of a different opinion, and held him in high esteem, and even had one or two secret conferences with him on the possibility of uniting both families by a marriage between her daughter and Mr Grantly's eldest son, who, as well as Arthur Melville, had their names enrolled for a foreign appointment as soon as there was a vacancy.

The friends all met at the station, and soon adieu was spoken, and hands warmly pressed, and the train moved on. Arthur Melville, though depressed with sorrow, was still buoyant with hope that before many months would elapse he might be in a fair way to gain the appointment; nor was he mistaken. And as we leave Alice and her friends to pursue their journey, we will follow his fortunes and see how varied they have been.

CHAPTER II.

CHRISTMAS came and went, and the tearful month
of April with its showers and sunshine, its opening buds and bright spring flowers, and Sandy
again was seated on the carriage-box driving to
the station.

Mr Melville was a proud man over his son's appointment, for Arthur along with Jim Grantly were appointed
to the Bombay and Calcutta bank respectively, Arthur
being sent to Bombay and Grantly getting charge of the
latter.

Varied feelings filled his breast as the carriage moved
away from the door of his childhood's home, and the many
familiar scenes and faces that met his gaze as he was being
driven along the London Road and past the Cross, as many
recollections and pleasurable associations crowded to his
memory, and, at what might be the last look of them, he
let fall a few manly tears. But even then the sunshine of
happiness was bursting through the cloud of sorrow that
looms at parting with those we love, for he thought of Alice
and how soon he might be able to claim her, and his heart
rejoiced.

As a matter of course, the two young men were to travel
together, and so took berths in the "Chaucer," a vessel
bound for Bombay, Grantly proceeding thence to Calcutta.

Professions of friendship existed between the two, and on Arthur's part was genuine, who in the fulness of his heart took the other into his confidence and recorded to him the story of his love and the bright prospect of having his hopes realised. How little he knew of the serpent heart, the demoniac hatred that lurked behind that fair exterior!

During the first part of the voyage the weather was favourable, and the ship made good headway, leaving dear old England's shores far behind. But there came a night, and a very terrible one, when even the oldest and most weather-beaten tars were hanging long faces, while the captain was giving directions in view of a coming storm.

The ladies being sent below, and out of danger as much as possible, only a few chose to remain on deck to watch the progress of the hurricane, Arthur and his companion being of the latter number. The ship began to heave fearfully with the heavy sea that was now running so as to make it necessary for those on deck to hold on by ropes, as it was becoming dangerous to every one unaccustomed to rough it.

Suddenly the vessel gave a great lurch, which caused our hero to lose his hold and fall heavily on the deck. A malignant smile of triumph crossed the face of Grantly as Arthur lay stunned and bleeding by his side. His evil angel whispered, and the dark deed was put into execution. Darkness closing in, and all hands being aft, while the few remaining loungers crept below being awed by the violence of the storm, Grantly seized the opportunity, lifted the prostrate Arthur, and having superior strength of limb and muscle, threw him overboard. Scarcely had he done so than the hypocrite sang out an alarm, tho' no one could either hear or attend.

Soon one of the masts fell with a crash. The elements threatened speedy destruction, but, happily, the storm was of short duration, tho' of terrific violence while it lasted.

Great was the damage done to the good ship, and it was feared the passengers and crew would have to abandon her and betake themselves to the boats, but relief was not far away; and as the morning dawned—the storm having subsided—a sail was discovered in the distance, to the joy of the many weary hearts who spent such a night in watching.

Soon they were all safe aboard a splendid vessel bound for Madras, where they arrived in due time. Grantly proceeded straight to his father's residence, as he held a responsible office in that city.

Mrs Moreland and her daughter had removed from Cawnpore, and were also at Madras; her son's regiment having been ordered more than a hundred miles inland.

Everything seemed to prosper with the Grantly's; the son meanwhile going to Calcutta. Many were the congratulations he received at his narrow escape, and great was the grief of Alice at Arthur's sad fate, for Grantly let her know of his death, and of the deep grief that filled his own heart at the loss of such a friend, and so managed to ingratiate himself with both mother and daughter with his false tongue, leaving his father to manage the rest; and an able ally he proved to be along with Alice's mother. But when the proposition was made to Miss Moreland, she recoiled at the idea that Jim Grantly should take the place of her Arthur, and it required threats as well as entreaties to make her give a reluctant consent. And her distrust of both father and son increased the nearer it came to the wedding-day, her mother urging on the preparations, where, for the present, we will let them remain and follow the fate of Arthur Melville.

CHAPTER III.

HEN Arthur was thrown overboard, he was sensible it was Grantly who committed the dastardly deed. He did not sink, as would be thought—thanks to the precaution of his excellent father, who provided him with one of Scheffer's life-preservers, the best then extant, and which he, during the voyage, carried about with him. The water revived him, and, in his despair, he gave himself up for lost; but presently he felt as if some hard substance was drifting close to him, and he instinctively clutched it. It was the broken mast, and again his senses failed. How his life was preserved on that dreadful night he could never tell; he knew it was the intervention of an all-wise and over-ruling Providence.

When he regained consciousness he was on board the "Theresa," a Government ship bound for Singapore. After several days of delirium, bending over him was the kindly anxious face of the ship's doctor.

"Where am I?" were his first words. "What has happened that you are looking at me so?"

"Hush," was the reponse, "you must not talk."

Then Arthur, fixing his eyes on the speaker, murmured—"No, no; it cannot be Uncle David—and yet——"

"And yet it is just your Uncle David, my dear boy; but

you have been very ill, and you must keep quiet, for you are too weak to talk much yet." Then, holding a glass to his lips, said—" Drink this and then sleep, so that you may be able to answer some questions when you awake." He obeyed, and like a weary child sank into a refreshing and strength-giving slumber.

His uncle, anxious to see the result of his skill on his nephew, watched assiduously by his berth, and, to his delight and satisfaction, saw him awake with renewed strength and vigour almost incredible.

As days passed on he continued to gain strength, so that when the ship arrived in port he was well, though pale and worn-looking from recent illness.

Arriving in Singapore, Dr Melville intended at first to remain for a considerable time on the island, as his engagement on the "Theresa" ended with the voyage, but having now a new interest in his nephew's restoration, as it were, from the dead, on second thoughts, he decided visiting several friends and relatives in the Indian Empire, and, among others, his sister, Mrs Moreland and her daughter, but first took a tour inland before proceeding to her former home, situated near the Bay of Bengal, as he thought his sister still resided there, though she had some-time before removed to Madras. Suffice it to say that several months elapsed before he arrived in that part of the country with his nephew, who was now perfectly restored to health and appeared more handsome than ever.

It may be mentioned here that owing to Dr Melville's sea-faring life his movements were generally unknown to his friends even for months together, so no one wondered when he turned up here or there unexpectedly, as in the present case he did, and, as he said to Arthur, he wished to doubly surprise them by not letting them know of his existence till they saw him once more in the flesh.

Disappointment at not finding Mrs Moreland in her former residence, they, after making inquiries as to her whereabouts (rather a difficult task in India) obtained the information, and were to proceed to Madras after a day's rest, and entering a " choultry," or travellers' rest, Dr Melville was trying to console Arthur with a promise to proceed as early as expedient, when, taking up a newspaper, was aimlessly looking it over, and was startled by the following :

"Important Announcement.—We understand that Mr James Grantly, manager of the Calcutta Bank, Limited, and son of Horace Grantly, Esq., Government Secretary, Madras, is about to lead to the altar Miss Alice Moreland, only daughter of the late Colonel Moreland of the Royal Bengal Fusiliers. The lady is possessed of rare beauty and many accomplishments, while the wealth possessed by her intended husband makes the marriage in every respect desirable. We wish them both much joy."

The paper dropped from his hand, and Arthur, alarmed at his uncle's unusual perturbation, sprang to his side, lifting the paper and read it also.

His heart sank within him, though he uttered no word ; but his energetic uncle soon regained his equilibrium. An old sailor was not to be so duped. Where did Grantly's wealth come from ? This was a question, with a little enquiry, he thought he could solve, as he had learned only a few days before that the assistant manager of the said bank was arrested and in jail for forgery.

" Poor Frazer," he thought, " you are the victim, but I know he is the villain. This solves the problem too of his attempt on Arthur's life, but I'll foil him yet. Then aloud he said, " Come Arthur, we must be going ; no time now to lose : cheer up, my boy, be quick, and Alice may yet be yours."

Cheered and encouraged Arthur obeyed, and soon they were learning particulars and giving information as to the conduct of so choice a scoundrel. Everything was done cautiously, and all evidence seemed to revolve itself in the form of guilt on the shoulders of Jim Grantly. Slowly did the Doctor proceed, to the great annoyance of his nephew, who was all impatience to be at his journey's end, but as surely did he spread the net for the unwary and now self-confident fool. The marriage was to take place on the 10th of June ; it was now the 8th, and as they neared the scene of their intended triumph, they kept themselves almost entirely disguised.

Great bustle and excitement prevailed at Upas Mount, the residence of the bride's mother. Everyone was gay and appeared to be happy, but poor Alice.

Mrs Moreland, fascinated by the handsome face and bland manners of the bridegroom elect, was really angry with her daughter for her caprice and self-will, as she was pleased to term it, so that she was in truth forced into submission.

All being ready, on the morning of the 10th a great number of guests arrived, and among the rest a special private carriage containing several gentlemen, who demanded of the porter a private apartment, with the injunction to tell them as soon as the clergyman made his appearance. We need scarcely say that these were none other than Dr. Melville, Arthur, and a few necessary for the unfolding of their plans.

The clergyman being announced, four of the gentlemen entered the drawing-room, and were not recognised among the crowded guests.

The bride, sad, and pale as a lily, looked beautiful even in her sadness. The bridegroom, with head erect and a smile of self-satisfaction curving his lips, was vaunting to himself how well he had planned and how near completion were all his schemes. The minister was about to begin the beautiful marriage service of the Church of England, when an elderly gentleman stepped forward and forbade the marriage, while another by his side put his hand on Grantly's shoulder and arrested him in the Queen's name.

" For what ? " he roared, fierce with passion.

" For robbing the Calcutta Bank and furthering your own ends with the money, and also for accusing an innocent man. See, here are the proofs ! "

" And, moreover, for the attempted murder of Arthur Melville," said the Doctor.

" 'Tis false ! " cried the wretch, trying to brave out the accusation by assuming the look of a bully. " He was washed overboard, and was drowned. I defy you all."

Here Arthur, at the Doctor's bidding, stepped forward, and at sight of him Grantly would have fallen had not the messenger-at-arms supported him.

" Do your duty," said Dr Melville to the Superintendent, who, being assisted by two of his subordinates, who were in waiting outside, Jim Grantly was marched off to the jail that William Frazer had vacated, there to await his trial for robbery and attempted murder.

Alice, who during the first part of the scene stood pale and trembling, yet retained her self-possession till Arthur appeared.

At sight of him she seemed oblivious to all around, and, with a glad cry, sprang to his outstretched arms and hid her face on his bosom, shedding happy tears.

She was conducted to her chamber by her bridesmaids,

who deeply sympathised with the bride, and gave vent to their opinions in no measured terms against any powers being predominant over a lady who wishes to marry the man of her choice, or to remain single if she chose—Mrs Moreland and old Grantly having a share of those comments.

Old Grantly, who had been indisposed for some weeks, had not been able to be present at this intended marriage of his son, and hearing of the turn affairs had taken succumbed, and in a few days passed from the world where he was neither envied nor honoured. So we will drop the curtain on father and son, none lamenting their fate.

How can I depict the astonishment of the guests? There were rapid whisperings on every side, asking what was the meaning of it all? But Dr Melville gave them to understand, in a few well-chosen words, the whole affair, adding there was no reason why they should disperse, as he expected the marriage would still go on, as there were both a bridegroom and groomsman, at the same time introducing Arthur and Mr Frazer to the wondering throng. "Then," he added, jocularly, "my esteemed sister, Mrs Moreland, and myself will undertake to give the bride away, and to dower her as well. Neither she nor her husband shall be portionless."

Mrs Moreland the while could scarcely hide her chagrin but smiled and bowed to her brother's proposal.

A burst of applause followed this announcement, and in a short time the ceremony proceeded. Arthur Melville and Alice Moreland were made one, all the dearer to each other for the trials they had undergone.

CHAPTER IV.

CHRISTMAS Eve again, and, at Irvineside Villa everything portends rare Christmas cheer. Mrs Melville and her two daughters are arranging leaves of holly and scarlet berries, with sprays of mistletoe, to conclude the Christmas decorations, while Mr Melville dogged in his easy chair. Presently he awoke, and asked Miss Melville to play "The March of the Harlech Men," a tune he was very fond of.

"I feel a little nervous to-night," he said. " I cannot account for the strange feeling, but I was dreaming of Arthur. I think that music will soothe me, so give us that, Katie, dear ; I like it so much, but I cannot get Arthur out of my vision to-night. It's strange ! very strange !"

Katie sat down, and, with her usual skill, ran her fingers over the prelude, when the violent ringing of the door-bell startled them, and the servant entered with a telegram.

Mrs Melville tore it open, and read as follows :—" Dr Melville, Gravesend, to George Melville, Irvineside Villa, Kilmarnock : ' Arrived at Gravesend ; expect me to dinner to-morrow along with other two friends.' "

" Uncle David is coming," cried little Maggie ; " dear darling old uncle David, and, clapping her hands, danced round the room in childish glee."

And every one was glad to welcome the dear old bachelor

uncle, though a shade had cast itself over the brightness of
the household since the reputed death of Arthur, and
particulars being kept back by the express command of this
same uncle, who delighted in surprising everyone as much
as possible. The Melvilles did not know the truth of the
case, and though some reports of Grantly's interference in
money matters had reached them, they were not so interested in them as they otherwise might have been.

Christmas day brought another telegram, reporting that
Dr Melville and his friends might be late for dinner, and
that they should not wait for them. Knowing six o'clock
was the well-known dinner hour on all occasions, no special
train being mentioned, no one met them at the station, so
they were enabled then to enter the house without being
observed by the guests.

Dr Melville knowing all corners, led the way to his room,
and being first ready, as was arranged between the three,
he proceeded to the dining-room while the two followed.
There a cordial reception awaited them. The Doctor
entered alone, and after the usual salutations on Christmas
he was pressed to sit down, which invitation he declined,
saying, "I must first produce my Christmas gifts. Here
they are," said he; "take to your arms once more your son
and daughter."

We need not depict the scene. Smiles and tears, joy
and grief were all blended together, for as yet they could
scarcely shake off the latter feeling; but thankful and happy
hearts knelt round the family altar that evening.

Old Sandy shed tears of joy when he welcomed his young
favourites home again. "Oh, man, Arthur," said the old
man, in the exuberance of his joy, "dae I see richt wi' my
auld een. I thocht ye was deid, and I mourned ye sair,
and I often thocht o' puir Miss Alice and hoo she wad be,

but noo that I see ye baith here, hale and weel, I canna think it true. Ah! but we're short-sichted mortals; but I kent, though Grantly had the cunnin' o' the verra deil, he wad only get the length o' his tether, and maybe no a' that either. I'm sae prood and happy, I wis' I cud leeve lang eneugh to serve ye, as I did baith yer faithers afore ye."

Though less demonstrative, not less heart-felt was the welcome given by the other servants; but such a season of gladness and festivity enjoyed by young and old is seldom witnessed as was enjoyed by all at Irvineside Villa on this special occasion.

The good Doctor took up his abode with his young friends, and lived a useful and happy life until a few years ago, when he caught cold, and to the great grief of his friends, was carried to the grave.

Mr Melville and his excellent wife, mother, and mistress, also sleep sweetly in the New Cemetery. Old Sandy, too rests not far from where his honoured master and mistress are laid.

Now nearly a quarter of a century has elapsed since the marriage of Arthur and Alice, and though they have had their share of joy and sorrow, shadow and sunshine, they are still happy and confiding as ever, love gilding and making sacred every action of their lives.

And now, wishing them and our readers a happy New Year, we say farewell.

The Fate of Nelly M'Neil.

[The main incidents of this Story are actual occurrences which have come within the writer's knowledge—names of persons and places being, of course, altered.]

CHAPTER I.

IT was a bright morning in the month of May, in the year 1860, when Nelly M'Neil stepped out of her father's cottage in the village of Dundonald, dressed in her new summer Sunday clothes, looking as bright and fresh as the morning itself. She was followed by her proud and fond mother, who stood in the doorway gazing after her with that admiration which only a mother can bestow, as Nelly stooped to cull a flower from the bed as she passed.

"When will ye be comin' hame, Nelly?" asked her mother. "I suppose it'll depend a guid deal on hoo ye'll fin' Annie; but if she be'na ony better ye'll just better bide wi' her till she's a' richt, tho' I'll miss ye sair eneuch."

"If I'm no hame the morn's nicht, mither, I'll write ye a line and tell you hoo she's keepin'," replied Nelly; "but I maun awa noo or I'll no be in Fenwick till it's far in the day."

And so bidding her mother good morning, Nelly tripped lightly out to the highway and betook hersel' to her journey in the best of spirits. For though she knew that her sister was ill, perhaps dangerously so, yet there was a joy that counterbalanced the grief in the thought that she would have an opportunity of meeting James Doeg, a thriving young farmer, who had won the pure and first love of her young heart.

Her sister, Annie M'Neil, had been adopted by an uncle who resided in Fenwick, and had been brought up by him from the age of seven years, and was the apple of his eye, as much as Nelly was the favourite of her parents; and though the sisters were always glad to see each other, yet there was not that binding love uniting them which generally exists betwixt those who are reared beneath the same roof. So Nelly was more overjoyed at the thought of seeing the object of her affection than of meeting and tending her sister.

Her mother stood for some time looking after her, and as she turned to re-enter the house she sighed and murmured, "God bless my bairn; she's a dear, bonnie lassie." Ah! how little she thought that her Nelly was gone from her for ever.

Having arrived at her destination, Nelly found Annie much better than she supposed her to be, but weak and looking thinner than she had ever seen her. The old housekeeper told Nelly that Annie had been "rale bad, but the doctor said she was oot o' danger noo, but care maun be ta'en o' her that she'll no tak' a backgaw, and she maun keep up her speerits,"—adding, as she looked knowingly at Annie, "I'm thinkin' if Jamie Sinclair was here she wud try and luik a wee brichter."

"Jamie Sinclair," said Nelly, "is to be hame sune, if he's

no' already in Glasgow. Sae ye'll better luik nervy, Annie,
and put on as blythe a face as ye can and no be haddin'
back the weddin', for I wud like to see ye awa' first, ye
bein' the auldest."

"And is yer ain waddin' sae near haun' when ye're
speakin' like that, Nelly," said Annie, with a deep blush.

"Aweel," returned Nelly, now blushing in her turn,
" I'm expectin' it'll no' be awfu' lang, for Jamie Doeg was
doon seein' my faither, and I ken for what."

A shade came over the good old housekeeper's face, while
she answered rather sadly, "Dinna ye put muckle faith in
Doeg, Nelly; I hae been hearin' queer things aboot him
that he's no a' thegither what he sud be."

"Ah! but ye maunna mind a' the ill tales ye hear,
Mysie," said Nelly. "Dae ye no min' when Annie's Jamie
got sic an awfu' bad character, an' whaur'll ye fa' in wi' a
dacenter lad?"

"Weel, Nelly, I'll no' say ony mair," said Mysie, "for
youth is aye houpfu' and 'ill no be convinced; but seein's
believin', Nelly, and noo I'll lea' ye and Annie till I get
the tatties poored, for yer uncle 'ill be in frae the kirk, and
he'll be needin' his dinner." And so saying she left the
room, and let the sisters discuss their love affairs alone.

CHAPTER II.

"ANNIE," said Nelly, "what dae ye think o' what Mysie has been sayin' about Jamie Doeg?"

"I haena paid muckle attention til't at a'," replied Annie, "but I heard my uncle sayin' that Flora Sinclair was awfu' muckle thocht o' wi' him, and that her father was unco keen for the match."

"But that's no' sayin' that Jamie wants her for a wife, though he thinks a lot o' her," returned Nelly, "but I'll e'en gang doon that way in the afternoon, and I'll maybe ha'e a chance o' seein' and speakin' a word or twa to him. I ken the stories are no' true, Annie. Fouk are unco fond o' crackin', and they'll get something mair to crack aboot after they see us thegither."

How true were the words, as the sequel will show, and how little did either of the girls apprehend that which was so soon after to occur.

After dinner Nelly, with her uncle, went to Dargel Farm to inquire for Mrs Doeg, James's mother. And as she wished, and had hoped, she met the object of her affection without the slightest shape of distrust in her young heart as regarded his intentions. After remaining for a short time with Mrs Doeg, who was very infirm, they took their leave and were accompanied by Jamie home. After making kindly enquiries as to Annie's health, he was asked to stay to tea and spend the evening there, which he did, though now and again he betrayed a certain uneasiness when anything was broached concerning marriage, and by his curt answers showed, for the present at least, that the subject was distasteful to him.

After tea, as was the usual custom when he and Nelly were together, they walked out for an hour or so on the banks of the Drumtee. This evening Nelly was especially gay and happy, and it was often afterwards remarked by those who had met her that her eye was unusually bright and the flush on her cheek was deeper than they had ever before seen it.

After getting out of the village to the banks of the stream, they leisure walked along in the direction of Kilmarnock. Nothing was spoken for a time till Doeg at last broke the silence and said :—

"Weel, Nelly, I'm glad I ha'e an opportunity o' seein' ye the nicht, for I had something very particular to say to ye."

"Weel, Jamie," said Nelly, with a blush, "what dae ye wish to say me?" thinking, in her simplicity, that he wanted to hurry matters regarding their marriage, as she knew his old mother was growing so frail that she could not look after the affairs of the house without the aid of some one.

Jamie did not immediately reply, and his silence boded no good to Nelly. At last he stammered out that he "scarcely kent hoo to begin," as if his guilty conscience was its own accuser, knowing the pure love he had received from Nelly, and how vilely he was about to recompense it by an act as cruel as it was deceitful.

As for Nelly, she felt as if some evil tidings were to be revealed to her, for she caught hold of his arm and said, "Tell me, Jamie, what's wrang, for ye're no like yersel' the nicht."

" Weel, I'll just tell ye in twa words, for there's nae use in makin' ony adae aboot it. This is the last time we can meet, Nelly, as I'm gaun to be marrit sune, for my mither's frail, and yer owre young ; and lea'in' a' that aside, I want a wife wha'll ha'e something to bring hame to me. Sae I've luiked oot for ane, an' faun' her too, sae there's nae use in sayin' ony mair aboot it. I was wrang to gang near ye at a', Nelly, but as ye're a sensible kimmer I ken ye'll luik at things in the richt licht, for ye ken ye hae naething, and that wad hardly suit me in the meantime. But," continued he, " ye'll get mony a braw lad to gang after ye, for ye're a braw bonnie lass "—and he made an attempt to smile as he tried to take her hand, saying—" Let us pairt as freens, Nelly."

Nelly, who stood like one stupified during this heartless speech, was roused by the touch of his hand, and started as if she had been burnt, saying—" Dinna daur touch me, Jamie Doeg, no even wi' yer little finger. After what ye've said I widna marry ye. Is a woman's heart sae licht a thing wi' ye, that ye wad barter it for siller. Ye ken ye socht my love afore I wared it on ye, but ye can gang yer wa's ; I'll no fash ye. But tell her that's to bring ye sae muckle, that it's her siller ye want, and no hersel'. The puir lass, whae'er she may be, is sair to be pitied, for it's a fause black heart she's trustin'."

So saying she turned from him, and without a word left him to no very reflections. He stood staring after her till she was out of sight in the direction of Kilmarnock. Then turning, he took the opposite course and slowly walked homeward, muttering to himself, " It's a' owre at last, and I'm maist vexed, for I like her better than Flora Sinclair ; but the siller ! the siller !— she want's that."

CHAPTER III.

E leave Nelly on her way to Auld Killie, and return to the cottage of her uncle, William Morton, and Annie, her sister.

As the evening wore on there was no apprehension caused by the absence of Nelly, till about half-past nine o'clock, when old Mr Morton said, " I wid like if Nelly wad come in noo, sae that we may ha'e worship, for I like a' body to be in the hoose by nine o'clock on a Sabbath nicht, and Nelly kens that."

" It's no like Nelly," said Mysie, "for she is aye sae exack to her time, and that has aye been a quarter afore nine, but seldom if ever after it, tho' she is the nicht."

" They've maybe gane farrer than ordinar' without thinkin', and cudna get back at the usual time, for I think she was in better speerits at seein' Jamie Doeg than e'er I saw her afore," said Annie.

" Weel, weel," said the uncle, good-naturedly, "it isna ilka nicht they hae an opportunity o' seein' ane anither, and I'm no gaun to begin to flyte the nicht. It's twa or three months since she was here afore."

So thus conjecturing, another half-hour slipped away. Ten o'clock came, and then eleven, and still no Nelly. Mr Morton held prayers, and as there was still no appearance he began to be uneasy. and proceeded to Dargel Farm to see if Doeg had returned.

He found Jamie walking towards his own door from the garden, where he had been ensconced in the summer house, whither he had retired in no enviable frame of mind. After his interwiew with Nelly, on seeing old Mr Morton he started like some culprit, and would have evaded him if he could.

"I have come, Jamie," said Morton, to speir if ye ken ocht o' oor Nelly. She hasna come in yet, and we just thocht ye micht hae ta'en a langer daunder than ordinar'."

"Atweel," said Jamie, "we pairted about a mile doon the burnside and she was makin' for hame. Something seemed to gang wrang wi' her and she said she was gaun hame."

"It's a wonnerfu' strange thing that she wud gang hame withoot tellin' ony o' us. I scarce got a word o' her, and I'm sure neither Annie nor Mysie said oucht that cud offend her. Ye sud hae come up and telt us," said Morton severely.

"I thoucht ye a' kent, and that there was nae need," said the hypocrite.

"It's very strange," said her uncle; "but she'll get hame a' richt eneuch, or we'll sune hear aboot it." And so bidding Jamie good-night, he retraced his steps to his own cottage, wondering much what could have possessed Nelly in going off so suddenly. Had he been sharper he might have detected something in Jamie's voice and manner that would have enabled him to solve the mystery.

Annie and Mysie were very much surprised at the news, but Mysie being a woman of sense and experience, laid this to that, and drew her own conclusions. The truth of Doeg's infidelity had become apparent, and Nelly, being made acquainted with his intentions, had left for home rather then return and make explanations which would be painful to all. So each concluded that there was no danger, and felt assured of her safe arrival at home. And thus a week passed away.

Her parents, on the other hand, though not having received her promised letter regarding Annie's health, were not in the slightest way uneasy, thinking she was safely housed in her uncle's at Fenwick.

And now comes the question, What has become of Nelly?

Pretty late in the evening of the day on which she left home, the attention of two workmen of the Caprington Estate was attracted by the form of a woman in a recumbent position, by the side of the Irvine, leaning forward as if bathing her face or drinking from the river. On coming up to her they asked what she was doing there so late. She answered evasively, saying she had come a good bit, and as she had a mile or two to walk before she got home, she was just resting. Satisfied for the time with this answer, they passed on and intended returning the same way; but having met some acquaintances they forgot and took a more circuitous route home. And it was not till a week later, when the same too men found a lady's umbrella stuck in the soft bank about a dozen yards from the brink, that the whole sad truth rushed to their minds that the young person they had seen there the Sunday before had drowned herself.

Their conjecture was right; and the poor girl who had come to this melancholy end was none other than the cruelly-used, heart-crushed Nelly M'Neil.

Yet there was no direct evidence that such was the case, and on relating the circumstances and making known their suspicions, a great number only laughed at them for their pains, and but for the persistent determination of a Mr Chrystal, a Kilmarnock gentleman, the efforts of the two men to recover the body would have proved unavailing. But energetically superintending the operations himself, he had the water dragged all the way down to Gatehead, and and at last the remains of the hapless Nelly M'Neil were discovered.

The same day being the market day in Kilmarnock, several women belonging to Dundonald, Gatehead, and the various farms round about, were returning from the town, and the news having spread as to the finding of the body, many were the wonderings and conjectures as to who and what the young woman was.

Among others who were returning after marketing was Mrs M'Neil, the poor drowned girl's mother, and, as each was giving her opinion, she remarked :—

" Aye, and they say she is rale weel dressed and seems to be quite young too. But," she added, " it'll no be easy kennin' for it's noo nearhand a fortnicht sin' the men spak till her. Oh me! I'm wae for her puir faither and mither.'

" Aye," answered a neighbour, "it's a sair day for them if they're leevin'."

"I wonner what ha'e they dune wi' the corpse," chimed in a third.

" I heard it was carried to ane o' the sheds at the station," replied the second speaker, " and if some o' ye wad gang to see't wi' me we micht be able to tell something aboot her."

To this some objected, but the greater number were for going. So arriving at the station they obtained permission to see the corpse, and one after another went round trying to identify it.

At last one spoke and said :—

" What kind o' a bonnet has she on, Mrs Kay ? "

T

" A white straw bonnet wi' green ties," was the answer.

" No," said Mrs Martin, " it's white ribbons, and a white feather, and a green and white checked scarf wi' fringes."

A low cry escaped Mrs M'Neil ; then she asked :

" What kind o' dress and shoon has she ? "

The sheet was turned over, revealing a dark stuff dress, and from its peculiar make and the light shoes that were on the feet, the dreadful fact was made known to Mrs M'Neil that it was her own well-beloved and blooming Nelly. And with one piercing shriek of " My Nelly ! my Nelly ! " she would have fallen had not the strong arms of the man in charge held her.

No one who heard that heart-rending cry can forget it. The poor woman was carried into the stationmaster's house till she had recovered sufficiently to be sent to her home in Dundonald.

CHAPTER IV.

DURING the fortnight that intervened between Nelly's visit to Fenwick and the recovery of her body from the Irvine, Annie had so far recovered as to be able to go about her duties as usual. Hurt at what she thought Nelly's coldness and indifference, she did not write home or make any inquiries as to her sudden departure, and being happy in the company of young Sinclair, who had returned a few days after Nelly's visit, and who was pushing matters regarding his marriage with Annie, as he wanted to make her all his own before leaving the country again for a short time. No wonder, then, that the news of Nelly's fate appalled them. Mysie alone could solve the mystery. That Doeg had blighted Nelly's life was evident to her, but she kept her own counsel.

It was indeed a mournful little company that left Fenwick to attend the funeral at Dundonald. Doeg, though invited, excused himself by saying that the shock was too much for him, and so, wrapped in his cloak of hypocrisy, evaded close questioning as regarded his last interview with Nelly.

The funeral being over, and the dead laid to rest, all had to return to the world to perform the various tasks allotted to them, let them be pleasant or painful.

So Jamie Sinclair, the young lieutenant, and Annie were quietly married about a month after the mournful events just related. It was a sad party, but perhaps two faithful hearts were all the more closely united on account of the sadness and the cause of it.

After a short stay with his bride, Lieutenant Sinclair took his leave with sincere regret, and promised to come home at Christmas at latest, which hope of meeting so soon again they had both to rely upon for comfort.

James Doeg, after a decent show of pretended grief for Nelly M'Neil, lost no time in trying to gain a footing with Flora Sinclair. He had her father's mind on the subject before he broke off his engagement so unceremoniously with Nelly ; so now he thought that with a proper show of feeling he might attain to the object of his desire, for it cannot be called affection.

But Flora Sinclair had given her heart to another, who had given her his own in return. And she told Annie in confidence that if her brother came home at Christmas she expected a friend along with him, blushingly adding that she had promised to be his wife even though her father objected.

"And what are ye gaun tae dae wi' Jamie Doeg ?" inquired Annie.

"He just can do what he likes with himself," replied Flora. "I never gave him any encouragement. He can look out elsewhere."

However, Mr Sinclair, who was a wealthy Kilmarnock merchant, thought otherwise, and pressed Flora to come to terms with Doeg. She favoured him so far as to go on with marriage preparations, but took care to keep both Doeg and the wedding-day at a distance. Mysie had informed her of how Jamie had boasted of the wealthy wife he was about to marry, which made her all the more determinedly steel her heart to disappoint him.

But as month after month passed and Flora's marriage was still in the background, Mr Sinclair grew exasperated, and told her he would stand it no longer, so he fixed her wedding for the last day of the year, telling her that come what might she would be forced to marry Doeg, or leave his house for ever, poor and penniless.

It was drawing near Christmas, and both Annie and Flora watched the newspapers and read all the shipping intelligence with eager interest, living in suspense between hope and fear. But as yet there was no news of the " Belvedere." The year drew to a close, and with it the wedding day at hand. The hope in Flora's heart of ever being Roger Murray's wife died out, and she resigned herself to her fate.

The wedding night came at length, and Flora, arrayed in her bridal finery, though handsome, looked weary and worn. The company assembled and the ceremony had begun, when the door was thrown open and James Sinclair and Roger Murray entered the room.

Sinclair sprang forward.

" I forbid this marriage," he cried, in firm and resolute accents.

The guests stared. Mr Sinclair was speechless with anger, while Doeg tried to bully and rage.

" Here is my sister's betrothed," he continued, " and she will *not* be forced into a union which is detestable to her ; and besides, she will never marry a man who is virtually a murderer ; for what else caused the death of Nelly M'Neil but his heartless rejection of her, with Flora Sinclair's hand and wealth in view. Begone, sir, or I will not be responsible for my behaviour towards you," he added, turning to Doeg, and the latter, with a cry of rage and shame, hurried out into the night.

"Go on with the ceremony, Mr Shortland; here is the bridegroom with all the preliminaries ready."

Every one was too much astonished to speak, and the clergyman, after a second injunction from James, made Roger Murray and Flora Sinclair man and wife, no one daring to object.

Explanations were soon forthcoming, and the man made aware how nearly he had been duped, for Doeg's affairs were found to be in a very bad state, some of his horses and cattle having died, which reduced his circumstances, so that he was fain to mend his fortune at any price.

Being baulked in this, he left his farm to take care of itself, and his old mother to do as she thought fit, and as she did not long survive the time of which we write, we will drop the curtain, beseeching those who would tread in evil's path for the sake of gain to remember the word of truth—"Be sure your sin will find you out."

THE END.

www.ingramcontent.com/pod-product-compliance
Lightning Source LLC
Chambersburg PA
CBHW031400270326
41929CB00010BA/1267